SUDAN
in Pictures

Francesca Davis DiPiazza

TF CB

Twenty-First Century Books

Contents

Lerner Publishing Group realizes that current information and statistics quickly become out of date. To extend the usefulness of the Visual Geography Series, we developed www.vgsbooks.com, a website offering links to up-to-date information, as well as in-depth material, on a wide variety of subjects. All of the websites listed on www.vgsbooks.com have been carefully selected by researchers at Lerner Publishing Group. However, Lerner Publishing Group is not responsible for the accuracy or suitability of the material on any website other than www.lernerbooks.com. It is recommended that students using the Internet be supervised by a parent or teacher. Links on www.vgsbooks.com will be regularly reviewed and updated as needed.

Twenty-First Century Books
A division of Lerner Publishing Group
241 First Avenue North
Minneapolis, MN 55401 U.S.A.

Website address: www.lernerbooks.com

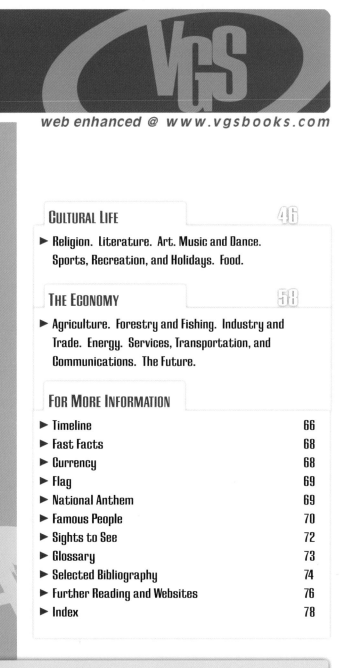

web enhanced @ www.vgsbooks.com

Library of Congress Cataloging-in-Publication Data

DiPiazza, Francesca Davis.
    Sudan in pictures / by Francesca Davis DiPiazza—Rev. and expanded.
      p.   cm. — (Visual geography series)
    Includes bibliographical references and index.
    ISBN-13: 978-0-8225-2678-0 (lib. bdg. : alk. paper)
    ISBN-10: 0-8225-2678-6 (lib. bdg. : alk. paper)
    1. Sudan—Pictorial works—Juvenile literature. 2. Sudan—Juvenile literature. I. Title. II. Series.
DT154.67.D515 2006
962.4'0022'2—dc22   2005017328

Manufactured in the United States of America
1 2 3 4 5 6 - BP - 11 10 09 08 07 06

INTRODUCTION

In July 2005, hundreds of thousands of people turned out in the Green Square of Khartoum, Sudan's capital city. They were there to witness and celebrate the public meeting of two longtime enemies: John Garang and General Omar Hassan al-Bashir. For two decades, the men had been on opposing sides of a long and bitter civil war. Garang was a southern rebel leader. Al-Bashir was the president of Sudan and was in charge of the northern army. But now they had come together to form a new government for Sudan.

The Republic of the Sudan had been torn by civil war since 1983. The south is largely rural and agricultural. The people of southern Sudan are mostly Black Africans who follow Christianity or traditional African religions. Since the nation's independence from Great Britain in 1956, southerners have struggled against the dominance of the more industrialized north. Northern Sudanese are mostly Arabs who follow the Islamic religion. A main factor in the struggle was the northern government's application of Islamic law

to all of Sudan, even to people and areas that were not Islamic.

Civil war and its effects, including starvation, has led to the deaths of more than 2 million Sudanese. Conflict has displaced more than 4 million people. Villages have been destroyed, and people are unable to grow their own food or earn money. Lack of investment in the south has led to lack of schools and basic health care. Young people have grown up without education or cultural traditions.

But in 2005, Sudan began what many hope is a new era. That year Garang and al-Bashir signed the Comprehensive Peace Agreement. They agreed to form a new government that represents both the north and the south, and to share power and wealth equally among the Sudanese people. John Garang was sworn in as vice president in July 2005, the first southerner to hold such a high post. Al-Bashir welcomed him, and together the two men signed an interim constitution. The new constitution guarantees that Islamic law will not be applied to the south. It also establishes freedom of religion and

freedom of expression. Yet, three weeks after being sworn in, John Garang died in a helicopter crash. His premature death created great uncertainty about the future of Sudan. However, despite initial riots, leaders throughout the country called for renewed commitment to peace. President al-Bashir pledged that the peace process would proceed as planned.

Excitement over the peace agreement was dampened by an ongoing, separate war in the west of Sudan. In the region of Darfur, thirty ethnic groups, all Islamic, have a history of competition for scarce resources, such as land and water. The ethnic tensions erupted into violence in 2003. Hundreds of thousands have been killed or have died from starvation and disease. More than one million have lost their homes and their livelihoods. The United Nations (a world peace-keeping organization) declared the situation in Darfur to be the largest humanitarian disaster in the world.

Sudan is Africa's largest country, covering 8 percent of the continent. The northern third of the country is mostly a sand and gravel desert where few people live. The central third of the country is mostly dry grassland. The south is tropical, with plains, forests, and swamps. The Nile River is the lifeline of the country. Its two main branches, the White Nile and the Blue Nile, meet at Khartoum. The Nile's fertile floodplain allows for agriculture. The river provides water and transportation and communication routes. River dams provide hydroelectricity.

Sudan's different landscapes are matched by many different ethnic groups, speaking more than one hundred languages. The nineteen major groups can be divided into hundreds of subgroups. The main political divisions are between Arab and non-Arab groups, but the country is far more complex than that.

Sudanese people sometimes describe the makeup of their country as *laham ras,* or "head meat." This term refers to the many separate tastes, textures, and looks of the different parts of a cooked sheep's head, a popular dish in Sudan. This diversity could be a great strength to the nation, or it could continue to tear it apart. If peace can unify the country, it will still take many years to rebuild and to repair the destruction from decades of war. The 2005 peace treaty between north and south is an important stride toward peace for all of Sudan.

THE LAND

Sudan occupies 967,500 square miles (2,505,825 square kilometers) in northeastern Africa, making it the largest country in Africa. It is as big as all of the United States east of the Mississippi River. Sudan's neighbors are Egypt to the north, the Red Sea on the northeast, Eritrea and Ethiopia to the east, Kenya and Uganda to the south, Democratic Republic of the Congo (Congo) and the Central African Republic (CAR) to the southwest, Chad to the west, and Libya on the northwestern corner. Saudi Arabia lies across the Red Sea.

Sudan's land is divided into three regions: deserts in Northern Sudan, semiarid plains in Central Sudan, and swampy and tropical areas in Southern Sudan. Most of the country is flat, but highlands and low mountain ranges rise at the eastern, southern, and western borders.

◉ Northern Sudan

Desert dominates Sudan's northernmost region. Few people live there. The Nile River flows north in an S shape through the desert. A narrow

green ribbon of land hosts many tiny villages up and down the Nile. On Sudan's northern border, the Nile enters the southern third of Lake Nasser. This huge lake formed when Egypt built the Aswan High Dam in the 1960s. The Nubian Desert lies to the east of the Nile River. To the west is the Libyan Desert, a section of the Sahara that covers most of North Africa. Gravel plains and shifting sands characterize the desert landscape. There are few oases (fertile, watered spots). Nomads—desert dwellers who move from place to place—draw water for themselves and their herds at a few small watering holes in the Libyan Desert. In the Nubian Desert, pyramids half-buried in sand are remnants of the once great Nubian civilization.

The Sahel, a wide belt of semiarid (semidesert) land, gradually emerges from the southern edge of the desert. The region has just enough rainfall to support some hardy plants, animals, and people.

In northeastern Sudan, the Red Sea Hills rise to peaks of up to 7,000 feet (2,134 meters) above sea level. The valleys of these dry hills support scrub vegetation in the north and dense growth near the Eritrean border. The coastal plain of the Red Sea, below the hills, is dry and rocky.

Central Sudan

A plain of grasslands known as savanna covers much of central Sudan. The plain is composed of clay soil, also known as cracking soil because it cracks during the dry seasons. The plain stretches southward from the capital city of Khartoum, at the junction of the White Nile and the Blue Nile. The fertile Gezira region is between these two rivers. It supplies Sudan with more than half of its agricultural income, which comes largely from cotton. The Marra Mountains mark the western end of central Sudan. Toward the center of the region, the plains rise to form the Nuba Mountains, a region of odd-shaped granite ridges. The easternmost part of central Sudan is grassland that stretches southward from Kassala.

Southern Sudan

Moving southward, rainfall increases gradually. Dense vegetation, shifting from grasslands to rain forests, covers Sudan's tropical southern region. Juba, the capital of southern Sudan, is in the far south. The White Nile spreads out above Juba into a vast swamp clogged with papyrus and floating water plants. This swamp—the world's largest—is called the Sudd (Arabic for "obstruction"). During high flood times, the Sudd exceeds 9,000

Jebel Marra, in the Marra Mountains, is the second-highest mountain in Sudan. It is an extinct volcano. Two lakes have formed in the crater.

LIBYA

EGYPT

SAUDI
ARABIA

*Lake
Nasser*

*Second
Cataract*

Nubian Desert

S a h a r a

N O R T H E R N   S U D A N

RED SEA HILLS

Libyan Desert

*Third
Cataract*

RED SEA

Nile River

*Fourth
Cataract*

*Fifth
Cataract*

Atbara River

Gash River

CHAD

*Sixth
Cataract*

ERITREA

MARRA
MOUNTAINS

C E N T R A L   S U D A N

GEZIRA

Blue Nile River

White Nile River

NUBA MOUNTAINS

S a h e l

INGESSANA
HILLS

Sobat River

ETHIOPIA

Sudd

CENTRAL
AFRICAN
REPUBLIC

IRONSTONE PLATEAU

S O U T H E R N   S U D A N

DIDINGA HILLS

DONGOTONA MTNS.

IMATONG MTNS.

Mount Kinyeti

KENYA

DEM. REP. OF THE CONGO

Sudan

Feet	Meters	
9843	3000	Mountains
6582	2000	Uplands
3281	1000	
1640	500	Lowlands

Elevation

N

UGANDA

International border
Mountain peak

0   200 Miles

0   200 KM

A F R I C A

SUDAN

ATLANTIC
OCEAN

INDIAN
OCEAN

0   1000 Miles

0   1000 KM

square miles (23,310 sq. km), making it as big as the state of Vermont. The Ironstone Plateau, located along the southwestern border, receives plenty of rain and has a long wet season. Tropical rain forests that begin here extend far into Congo. Sudan's southern ranges—the Imatong Mountains, the Dongotona Mountains, and the Didinga Hills—border Uganda. Within the Imatong range lies Mount Kinyeti, which, at 10,456 feet (3,187 m), is the highest peak in Sudan.

◉ The Nile River and Its Influence

The Nile River—including its main tributaries, the White Nile and the Blue Nile—is Sudan's most important geographic feature. The Nile is the longest river in the world, traveling south to north for 4,145 miles (6,671 km). Almost half of that distance is through Sudan. The land drained by the Nile is called the Nile Basin and includes the entire country of Sudan.

The White Nile starts in southern Uganda in Lake Victoria, its largest source. It enters Sudan just south of Juba. At Bor it enters the Sudd and wanders slowly north, losing about half of its water to evaporation. In 1978 the Sudanese government began building the Jonglei Canal to divert the river around the swamp. The canal would provide a transportation route and lessen evaporation. Civil war in the south, however, put a stop to construction in 1984. On the other side of the Sudd, the White Nile receives water from the Sobat River. The White Nile meets the Blue Nile, coming from the Ethiopian highlands, at Khartoum.

The yearly **flooding** of the Nile is important for creating fertile farmland in Sudan.

The two tributaries then form the main Nile River. North of Khartoum, the Atbara River also joins the Nile.

The seasonal flooding of the Nile River is vital to the lives of the Sudanese. The volume of water in the main Nile at the peak of the flood period (late August) is usually about sixteen times that of its lowest stage, which occurs in April. After the floods recede in the fall, the muddy river leaves behind silt (particles of dirt), creating fertile agricultural land. Altogether, the Nile irrigates about 2.8 million acres (1.1 million hectares) of land in Sudan. The remainder of the year, from January to mid-July, is the rest period, when the Nile does not provide enough water for irrigation.

When the Blue Nile comes pouring down from the highlands at flood season, it crashes into the slower White Nile at Khartoum. The waters of the White Nile back up for miles as the two rivers intermingle before continuing north. This dramatic scene is visible from the White Nile Bridge in Khartoum. From above, the different colors of the rivers can be seen. Due to different silts, the Blue Nile's water is clearer than the gray-colored White Nile.

Above Khartoum, the Nile slowly winds its way north. It drops little in elevation except at five cataracts, or rocky rapids, before it empties into Lake Nasser. The cataracts are numbered in ascending order from north to south.

Several dams on the Blue Nile, including the Rusayris Dam and the Sennar Dam, help regulate that river's flow and store floodwaters for irrigation. The Aulia Dam on the White Nile provides irrigation water to parts of central Sudan. Dams also harness the power of rushing water to create hydroelectricity, which supplies about 53 percent of Sudan's power. The government has scheduled ten more dams for completion by 2010.

Rainfall and Climate

The climate of Sudan corresponds roughly to its three main areas, becoming gradually cooler and moister from north to south. The desert climate is arid. Rain is rare—the desert usually gets no more than 4 inches (10 centimeters) a year. Dust storms are common. Central Sudan has a variable rainy season, receiving between 4 to 32 inches (10 to 81 cm) of rain each year. Except in drought years, rainfall provides this area with enough water to grow much of Sudan's food. Southern Sudan receives the largest amounts of moisture, with some places averaging 32 to 55 inches (81 to 140 cm) of rainfall annually.

The haboob is a dust storm or sandstorm that blows from the Libyan Desert. The hot, dry wind sweeps southward along the Nile, carrying huge clouds of dust that wither plants and coat the streets of villages and cities as far south as Khartoum. Fine particles of sand and dust get into buildings and clothes, as well as into people's eyes, noses, and mouths.

In the north, the Libyan Desert is one of the hottest places on earth. July average highs reach 110°F (43°C), and the thermometer may rise above 125°F (52°C). Average winter lows in the desert drop to 60°F (16°C). The temperature in the desert varies greatly between day and night. Nights may be as cold as 40°F (4.4°C), as there is no cloud cover to hold in the day's heat.

The central and southern regions benefit from rain and clouds that decrease temperatures in these areas. Temperatures in central Sudan are between 74°F (23°C) in January and 89°F (32°C) in July. Southern Sudan sees slightly lower averages. Mountain regions also tend to be cooler and moister than surrounding lowland areas.

Natural Resources and Environmental Issues

The Red Sea coast provides access to international shipping, but the Nile is Sudan's most important resource, providing water and fertile floodplains for agriculture. Nile perch and other fish are sources of protein. The river and its branches also provide transportation routes, and dams create hydroelectric power.

Sudan has four national parks, but war, refugees, and poaching (illegal hunting) have devastated them. Poachers slaughter elephants, for instance, for their valuable ivory tusks. Hungry people kill wildlife to eat and cut trees for fuel. Loss of habitat and overhunting have threatened thirty-three animal species in Sudan with extinction.

Leading mineral resources are iron ore, copper, chromium ore, and gypsum. The Red Sea Hills have a high gold content. In the 1970s, oil companies discovered petroleum in the south and southwest, but civil war has disrupted full development of oil fields.

Sudan suffers from serious droughts, or periods of insufficient rainfall. In the 1990s, Sudan was on the United Nations' list of most severely drought-affected countries. Rainfall has improved in the twenty-first century, but drought remains a serious concern.

Desertification, or the process of land becoming barren, is another environmental challenge in Sudan. Lack of rain is compounded by overuse of dry lands, such as in the Sahel, where more people grow crops and graze animals than the environment can support. Almost 12 percent of Sudan's land is forested, but most trees are harvested for fuel, not timber. Wood gathered for fuel destroys trees that hold the soil in place, and wind blows the soil away. Scientists believe that

Most of northern Sudan is **desert.** Summer temperatures in the desert can reach as high as 125°F (52°C).

THE DESERT FOX

The tiny fennec, also called the desert fox, roams dry lands mostly at night, hunting rodents and other small animals. The body fluids of its prey provide the fennec with all the water it needs. It spends the heat of the day burrowed deep under the sand. The light buff color of its fur reflects the heat of the sun and provides camouflage. Large ears help this hunter hear at night. They also help the fox stay cool. The animal's blood loses heat as it circulates through the thin skin of the ears.

Sudan's deserts—along with the rest of the Sahara, which already covers as much land as the mainland United States—are spreading.

Simple, inexpensive projects (such as planting tree seedlings) reduce desertification. But conflicts and war intensify Sudan's environmental issues. Money and human energy that could be spent protecting the environment have gone to military use. Millions of people have become refugees in their own country and are no longer able to care for their land.

◉ Flora and Fauna

In the desert areas, vegetation grows only around a few oases and along the Nile. Date palm and citrus fruit trees are two types of vegetation that grow in desert regions. Date palms are an important source of food and building materials. In the Sahel, small, thorny trees, mainly acacia, appear among grasses and other low, scrubby plants. Various types of grasses sprout during periods of rain, but these quickly wither away after the rains end. South of this zone, the true savanna begins, forming areas of permanent grass with a scattering of trees. Baobab trees, which conserve water in their giant trunks, are a fairly common sight.

In the Sudd, the most common plant is papyrus—a marsh plant that grows up to 10 feet (3 m) tall. In the southern forests, typical trees are the giant mahogany, the tamarind, and the sausage tree—so called because of the sausagelike appearance of its edible fruit. Near the southern borders, the terrain ranges from thick rain forest to open, parklike country, where acacias, scrub vegetation, and high mountains provide a variety of animal habitats. Elephants, hyenas, lions, giraffes, buffalo, and many varieties of antelope live in the south. Termites, beetles, and ants are common insects. Mosquitoes and tsetse flies spread diseases.

Animals in savanna lands include wild sheep in northern Darfur and ibex (wild goats) in the Red Sea Hills. Domesticated animals, such as goats, have mostly replaced large grazing animals, such as giraffes, and large predators, such as leopards. Smaller animals including

Aardvarks are found in Sudan. The aardvark uses its strong claws to burrow in the earth. Termites are its main food. For more photos and information on the wildlife of Sudan, visit www.vgsbooks.com for links.

baboons, warthogs, and aardvarks are still common. Honey badgers—which despite their small size are one of the continent's fiercest predators—are also common. Birds such as larks and wheatears (a kind of thrush) eat bugs, while the short-toed eagle feeds on snakes. Buzzards eat the plentiful rodents, including jerboas and gerbils. Insect life includes beetles and butterflies. The Nile crocodile and the Nile monitor, a flesh-eating lizard, live along the Nile and its branches. The Nile perch lives in the waters of the Nile and often weighs more than 200 pounds (90 kilograms). Herons and cranes fish in the country's waters, and shoebills, storklike birds, live in the Sudd.

Some animals have adapted to life in the northern deserts. Reptiles, such as spiny-tailed lizards and snakes such as sand vipers, have an advantage in being cold-blooded. They warm up in the sun and cool off by burrowing under the sand. Their scaly skins also keep them from drying out. Small mammals do better than large ones in the dry, hot lands, and there are many kinds of rodents in the desert. They are nocturnal, or active at night, to avoid the hot sun, and they get most of their water from the plants they eat. Invertebrates (animals without a spinal column) in the desert include antlions (meat-eating ants) and scorpions. Birds and winged insects, such as desert locusts, fly long distances for food and water in the desert.

Al-Kabir Mosque, an Islamic house of worship, can be seen in the background of this busy city scene of **Khartoum.**

Khartoum

Sudan's capital, Khartoum, was built around the junction of the Blue Nile and the White Nile. The river runs between Khartoum, Omdurman, and Khartoum North. Bridges across the rivers connect the three cities, which have a combined population of about 3 million people. Drought, civil war, and unemployment have brought throngs of rural Sudanese to the capital in search of work. Overcrowded refugee camps on the outskirts of town house thousands of people in inadequate, unsanitary conditions.

In Arabic, the official language of Sudan, *Khartoum* means "elephant trunk." An early resident imagined that the curve where the Blue Nile meets the White Nile resembled the long snout of an elephant.

The modern city follows an easy-to-navigate grid with paved streets and wide boulevards. Buildings include traditional onion-domed mosques (Islamic houses of worship), high-rise apartment buildings, foreign embassies, and the University of Khartoum. Internet cafés offer online computer access for a small fee. A tree-lined walkway and riverside restaurants take advantage of the riverside setting. Omdurman hosts the country's largest souk, or outdoor market, and a camel market.

Secondary Cities

On the Red Sea coast, Port Sudan (population 450,000) is Sudan's only major industrial port. Most of Sudan's trade with other countries flows through the city's docks. Port Sudan is also a base for some of the Red Sea's best recreational diving. Ferryboats south of the city at the old port of Sawakin transport people across the Red Sea to Jidda, Saudi Arabia. Many faithful Muslims make this thirteen-hour trip on their annual pilgrimage to the holy city of Mecca.

On the border of Eritrea, Kassala (population 335,000) is the largest market town in the agriculturally rich east. It is connected to Port Sudan and Khartoum by Sudan's main highway and by rail. The city is located in the Kassala hills on the Gash River. An estimated 500,000 refugees from Sudan's civil war and Ethiopia and Eritrea's internal strife live in refugee camps around Kassala.

Juba (population 200,000) is located on the White Nile near the border with Uganda and Congo. War has reduced Juba to a town of mud huts. People wash in the Nile River, and no transportation system is available. The 2005 peace treaty, however, is bringing change, including the construction of new buildings, roads, and phone systems.

An old market town, Gedaref (population 191,000) has grown because of its location in a wide valley in eastern Sudan. The bowl-shaped landscape helps to collect a water supply that is sufficient for agriculture. Gedaref is the largest market in the country for millet (a type of grain), which is grown on a large scale in the district.

With a population of about 105,000, Atbara is the largest city on the Nile in the northern states of Sudan. It serves as a transit center for buses and trains. The small town of Dunqulah (population 18,400) is famous for its palm groves on the Nile. It also serves as a base to visit the ruins and sites of ancient Nubia.

Visit www.vgsbooks.com, where you'll find links to more information about Sudan's cities—including the climate and weather, population statistics, and more.

HISTORY AND GOVERNMENT

Because of geographical differences, Sudan's early history developed in two distinct ways. The northern and central regions of the nation, together called northern Sudan, had close ties with developments in Egypt and the Mediterranean and Arab worlds. The southern region developed a more isolated culture based on cattle herding and family and group loyalties. Geographically connected to central Africa, southern Sudan remained relatively undisturbed until the nineteenth century, when British colonial powers united the two regions into one political unit. Sudan's northerners and southerners continue to think of themselves as separate groups.

Early History

Archaeologists have found evidence of human settlements from eight thousand years ago in the Nubia region. The Nubia region begins at Khartoum and stretches north to the city of Aswan, Egypt. The name Nubia comes from "nub," the Nubian word for "gold." Nubian burial

sites were rich with artifacts such as gold jewelry and art objects, fig-
urines, pottery, and weapons.

Ancient Egyptian written records refer to the area now called Sudan.
These sources talk about the Cush region in northern Sudan. In about
2400 B.C., Kerma became the first kingdom in Cush. It competed with
Egypt to control trade with central Africa. Egypt captured Cushitic people
to use as slaves and eventually defeated and burned Kerma in 1500 B.C.

The ups and downs of Egyptian politics—when pharaohs (rulers or
kings) governed the region—touched Cush in various ways. When the
pharaohs were under siege in their own realm, Cush suffered less
interference from Egypt. On the other hand, powerful Egyptian rulers
sometimes brought the region of Cush within their control.

By the eighth century B.C., Cush had emerged as an independent
kingdom centered in Napata, near the rapids of the Fourth Cataract of
the Nile. The climate at that time was wetter, and the region had
plenty of grass and woodlands. Napatan kings called themselves

pharaohs and built pyramid-shaped tombs. The Egyptians subdued Napata in 590 B.C. and forced the kingdom to move its capital south to Meroë, near the river's Sixth Cataract, close to Khartoum.

The Meroitic kingdom is the most famous of the Cush kingdoms. Palaces, temples, and burial grounds from the kingdom are well preserved by the desert climate. At its height, Meroë had about 25,000 inhabitants. The wealth of the kingdom came from trade. Central Africa provided precious materials such as gold, copper, ivory, and ebony. Greek and Roman luxury items also came through Meroitic trading networks. Nubian traders were the first to use camels extensively for caravans (traveling groups). A number of queens, called *candace* (pronounced "kan-dah-kay"), ruled at Meroë. The kingdoms resisted domination by the Roman Empire, an empire that controlled much of the Mediterranean world. The Romans were stopped from conquering Nubia by the difficulty of traveling past the northernmost Nile cataract.

In A.D. 324, however, an army from the aggressive Aksumite kingdom of northern Ethiopia traveled west. The Aksum ruler, Ezana, was a Christian. His armies defeated Meroë, ending the Meroitic kingdom's independent existence.

The Late Nubian Kingdoms

With the decline of Meroë, smaller realms—Nobatia, Muqurra, and Alwash—took over the Nubian Desert area of northern Sudan. Some Nubians gradually adopted the Egyptian and Ethiopian form of Christianity. Ties with Christian Egypt brought the Nubian kingdoms into greater contact with Christian cultures around the Mediterranean

THE LION GOD

Ancient Nubians in the Meroitic kingdom (ca. 270 B.C.–A.D. 324) worshipped Apedemak, a god with the head of a lion. Nubians built temples with carved stone reliefs of the lion god, sometimes showing him with wings or with a snake body. Professor P. L. Shinnie translated into English this inscription (carved writing) to Apedemak:

"You are greeted, Apedemak . . . great god . . . lion of the south, strong of arm. . . . The one who carries the secret, concealed in his being. . . . Who is a companion for men and women . . . the one who hurls his hot breath against his enemy. You are called Great of Power. . . . The one who punishes all who commit crimes against him. . . . Who gives to those who call to him. . . . Lord of life. . . . "

——Marian Broida, *Ancient Egyptians and Their Neighbors* (Chicago: Chicago Review Press, 1999).

Sea. Friction between the Romans and the Nubians was frequent until the Roman emperor Justinian I sent missionaries to teach and preach Christianity (the religion of the Roman Empire) to Nubia in 543. Nubia was entirely Christian by 575.

In the early seventh century, a new religion arose across the Red Sea on the Arabian Peninsula. Islam, the religion of Muslims, was founded by the prophet (spiritual spokesperson) Muhammad. After Muhammad's death in 632, Arab Muslim armies threatened the security of the Christian Nubian kingdoms. These Arab forces conquered Egypt in 642. For their own safety, Nobatia and Muqurra joined together to form the kingdom of Dunqulah in about 700.

◉ Arab and Nilotic Arrivals

In the 700s, Arab armies entered Nubia bringing Islam with them. But Islam took hold very slowly in northern Sudan, where large numbers of Nubians practiced Christianity. Instead of converting the Christian Nubians, the Arabs decided to capture and sell them into slavery as servants or soldiers.

The Nubians resisted the Muslim armies and the new religion. Rather than fight a prolonged war, the Arabs arranged a series of treaties, or *faqt*, with the Nubian kingdoms. Under the treaties, the Nubians promised an annual quota of slaves in exchange for Egyptian goods and produce. The faqt governed relations between the Nubians and the Arabs for six hundred years. But the Nubians continued to resist the Arab armies, merchants, and religious leaders that streamed into the area.

In about 1000, African peoples of Nilotic (related to the Nile) ethnic groups migrated to the southwest of Sudan, in the area of the White Nile. Little is known of the early history of these peoples, the ancestors of the Dinka, Nuer, and other modern southern groups. They herded animals and grew crops on the grassy savannas. The base of their social organization was the family. Extended families formed units called clans. Each clan had its own leader, a role that often blended religious, priestly power with decision-making abilities.

Eventually, the Nubian kingdoms faltered as Islamic strength increased. Turkish Islamic soldiers called Mamluks conquered Dunqulah in the fourteenth century. The kingdom of Alwash collapsed in 1504, when the Funj sultans (Islamic kings) established the first Muslim monarchy in Sudan, with its capital at Sennar. After a long rivalry, in 1517 the Ottoman Empire—an Islamic empire that arose in Anatolia (modern-day Turkey)—gained control of Egypt and Nubia from the Mamluks. The Nubian form of Christianity, cut off from other Christian cultures, began to wither away. By the seventeenth century, it had disappeared.

▶ The Sultanate of Sennar and the Turkiya

The Funj was a loose collection of small realms that recognized the sultan of Sennar as their leader. The capital city was at the center of several trade routes in the region, which the sultanate (kingdom) protected for more than three centuries. In exchange for safe caravan routes, the small vassal (dependent) states contributed taxes and troops on a regular basis.

At the height of its power in the middle of the seventeenth century, the Sennar sultanate repelled attacks by non-Muslim African peoples from the south, by Ethiopian groups to the east, and by Arabs from the north. Because of its military success, the sultanate attempted to centralize its power in the seventeenth and eighteenth centuries. This move meant that the small vassal states would have less influence in the decisions that affected them. The resistance of the vassal states to centralization weakened the sultanate. By the early nineteenth century, the smaller realms had substantially loosened their ties to the sultanate of Sennar.

In 1811 Muhammad Ali Pasha—a high-ranking official of the Turkish Ottoman Empire in Egypt—conquered the declining sultanate of Sennar. He seized gold and forced black Africans to serve as soldiers for his regime. A second Egyptian army arrived in 1820 and firmly established Egyptian rule—called the Turkiya—in Sudan. In the decades that followed, the Egyptians greatly extended the boundaries of their new territory. Their control reached southward toward Uganda and west into Darfur.

Muhammad Ali Pasha made his plans clear after conquering Sennar. He wrote them in a letter to a commander: "You are aware that the goal of all our effort and this expense is to procure blacks. Please show zeal in carrying out our wishes in this supreme matter."

The early period of Turco-Egyptian rule proved harsh for the Sudanese. Officers of the occupying army demanded huge sums of money from the people who lived there, and the soldiers fed themselves from the food that people grew for their families.

The slave trade increased in order to restock the Egyptian army. Raiders traveled throughout the north, and fleeing populations left their fields untended. In search of slave recruits, hunters went into the southern reaches of Sudan, making contact for the first time with Nilotic groups. These peoples were greatly impacted by the slave trade and came to refer to it as "the time when the world was spoiled." Corruption and the slave trade created widespread unrest among the Sudanese under the Turkiya.

The Mahdi

In the 1880s, Muhammad Ahmad, the son of a boatbuilder from Dunqulah, began to preach against the corrupt rule of the Turkiya. He encouraged the Sudanese to drive the Turks from Sudan. Claiming descent from the prophet Muhammad, he called himself al-Mahdi al-Muntazar (the Awaited Guide in the Right Path).

Many people in the countryside began to view Muhammad Ahmad as the awaited guide, the Mahdi. When the government in Khartoum sought to arrest him, the Mahdi fled with his supporters to the region of Kurdufan. He gained the support of the nomadic cattle herders of Kurdufan and Darfur. Early in 1882, the Mahdi and his followers, by then thirty thousand strong, began an armed resistance against the Egyptian occupying forces. Also in 1882, Great Britain—the strongest world power at the time—took control of Egypt to protect vital trade routes in the region. In 1883 the Mahdi's forces won a battle at Shaykan, south of Khartoum, against ten thousand British-led Egyptian troops. The Mahdists gradually gained control over much of northern Sudan.

With the Mahdi's success, the British sent General Charles Gordon to Khartoum in February 1884 to withdraw the Egyptian troops from Sudan. Acting against his government's orders, Gordon maintained the Egyptian forces at Khartoum, believing he could eliminate the Mahdists. In response, the Mahdists attacked Khartoum. Public outcry in Britain to rescue Gordon pressured the British government into sending a relief force. The relief expedition arrived in Khartoum on

Muhammad Ahmad declared himself **the Mahdi** in 1881. Over the next four years, he led a successful war against the British-led Egyptian occupation of Sudan.

TRAPPED IN KHARTOUM

General Charles Gordon of Great Britain kept a journal while he was under siege in Khartoum. During an attack of the Mahdi's forces on November 12, 1884, Gordon recorded his feelings of dread at being awakened by the sound of the battle nearby:

"One tumbles at 3:00 A.M. into a troubled sleep; a drum beats—tup! tup! tup! It comes into a dream, but after a few moments one becomes more awake and it is revealed to the brain that *one is in Khartoum*. . . . Where is the tup, tupping going on? A hope arises it will die away. No, it goes on and increases in intensity. . . .

"Up one must get and go on the roof of the palace; then telegrams, orders, swearing and cursing goes on till about 9:00 A.M. . . . Men may say what they like about the glories of war, but to me it is . . . horrid. . . ."

Two months later, the Mahdi's forces took Khartoum and speared Gordon to death.
—John H. Waller, *Gordon of Khartoum: The Saga of a Victorian Hero*

January 28, 1885. But the Mahdi's forces had already won, and Gordon had been killed, despite the Mahdi's order that his life be spared. Six months later, the Mahdi died of typhoid fever.

After some internal fighting, a *khalifa*, or successor to the Mahdi, was chosen. Abdullahi, the Mahdi's first supporter, emerged as the khalifa, and his reign was known as the Mahdiya. Abdullahi had many challenges to face, since several European countries—including Germany, Italy, France, and Britain—wanted to claim territory in Africa for their colonial empires.

The Anglo-Egyptian Condominium

With the scramble for African colonies, British troops in Egypt hastened their occupation of Sudan in order to outpace the French. In 1898 Britain's General Horatio Kitchener defeated the Mahdists at the Battle of Omdurman. By 1899 a large chunk of land—called Anglo-Egyptian Sudan—was under Anglo-Egyptian control. The Condominium (co-rule) Agreement of 1899 established the joint authority of Britain and Egypt over Sudan.

Under the condominium, British officers had far-reaching powers. All executive authority—in the form of a council headed by the governor-general—was in the hands of the British. In addition, British laws began to control judicial decisions. Sharia courts—religious tribunals run by Islamic leaders—were allowed, but their decisions could not conflict with British law. Organized slave raids ended under British rule, but southerners continued to distrust

Arabs, and northerners continued to look down on southerners.

Government projects developed smoothly in northern Sudan. Telegraph and rail lines connected major regions of the north but did not reach remote areas at all. Port Sudan opened in 1906, and irrigation programs in the 1920s transformed large sections of central Sudan into farmland. The government spent less money to develop the south, although the area had good potential for agriculture.

European Influence in the South

Remote and underdeveloped, the southern states had most of their contact with Europeans through Christian missionaries. The missionaries operated health clinics and schools with instruction in English. Graduates of these mission schools began to fill civil service posts (jobs in government bureaucracy) in the south. In this way, the south's political power base developed from a Christian, English-speaking foundation, while in the north, Islam and Arabic prevailed within the bureaucracy.

With the intent of eventually combining southern Sudan with their East African colonies of Tanzania, Uganda, and Kenya, Great Britain actively encouraged the southern states to identify themselves with these countries. The government barred northern Sudanese from traveling to the south, and it prevented southerners from seeking employment in the more developed north. An announcement in 1930 decreed that southerners were to regard themselves as ethnically distinct from northerners.

Road to Independence

Amid these internal conflicts, two political parties emerged in Sudan in the 1940s. The National Unionist Party (NUP) favored union with Egypt, while the Umma Party wanted independence for Sudan. The British Empire was greatly weakened by World War II (1939–1945). After the war, Great Britain was gradually forced to give up its colonial holdings around the world. In 1948 the British established a Sudanese legislative assembly, or lawmaking body. In that year's elections, which the NUP boycotted, the Umma Party gained a majority of seats.

In 1953 the Egyptians and the British drew up a new treaty, paving the way for Sudanese independence. The NUP participated in the elections held in 1953 and won a clear majority. The NUP's leader, Ismail al-Azhari, formed a colonial government in 1954.

As the British turned more and more control over to the Sudanese, southerners saw signs of domination by the north. The new legislature chose Arabic as the official language of administration throughout

The **Sudan parliament** that was elected in 1953 met in Khartoum for the first time on January 1, 1954. The NUP held a majority of the seats.

Sudan. The former policy of isolating the southern states gave way to openness in the realms of trade and employment, and northerners began to take over key positions in the south, replacing traditional leaders. Furthermore, Muslims were no longer barred from trying to gain religious converts in the south. The southerners objected to these moves. They saw them as part of the government's "Arabization" campaign.

Independence and Its Aftermath

Although union with Egypt was the main idea in the NUP's political platform, antiunion riots and demonstrations convinced the al-Azhari government to change its position radically. Al-Azhari publicly announced that he was in favor of Sudanese independence and called for a withdrawal of foreign troops. The Sudanese legislature unanimously passed a declaration of Sudanese independence on December 19, 1955, and the nation formally became a self-governing republic on January 1, 1956.

After 1956 coalition (power-sharing) governments in Sudan found that their Western-style administrative methods did not work to unify a country with such diverse ethnic groups. Regional and religious ties were strong. Some of the southern groups, desiring self-rule, rebelled against the northern-led government's attempts to control them.

Internal conflicts—including the outbreak of civil war in the south—stagnated the political process and encouraged the army to take over the government of Sudan in 1958. A military council governed the country, expelling Christian missionaries in the south and seeking to resolve issues by military rather than political action. In 1964 a general strike in the country led to the restoration of civilian rule.

Starting in the late 1960s, the Sahel began to experience a series of severe droughts. Scientists believe this may be part of an ongoing worldwide climate change. Drought eventually began to cause food shortages in Sudan.

Civilian rule lasted until 1969, when a young military officer, Colonel Jaffar Nimeiri, assumed power in a second coup (sudden, often violent, overthrow of government). In 1971 Nimeiri was elected by general vote to a six-year term as president.

The Nimeiri Era and al-Mahdi

Nimeiri seemed to solve the problems of southern politics in 1972. At a historic meeting in Addis Ababa, Ethiopia, the Sudanese government agreed to give regional authority to the southern Sudanese. The civil war came to a halt, but Nimeiri still faced civilian disturbances led by various political and ethnic groups that disagreed with his policies. Frustrated by inflation, food shortages, and other economic hardships, these groups staged many public demonstrations. They wanted to expose the regime's inability to provide basic opportunities for Sudan's people. In 1974, faced with labor and student unrest, Nimeiri declared a state of emergency.

In the 1970s, oil was discovered in Darfur. It was not exploited because international oil companies left Sudan due to the country's instability.

A decade after signing the agreement in Addis Ababa, Nimeiri weakened the authority of the south by dividing the region into three parts. In 1982 he also imposed the strict Islamic law of Sharia throughout the country, whether or not people were followers of Islam. Legal punishments included amputation for theft, public lashings for alcohol possession, and stoning to death. This was controversial even among

NUBIA UNDERWATER

In 1960 the Egyptian government began building a huge dam on the Nile at Aswan. They knew the dam would create an enormous lake stretching into Sudan. The lake would cover most of northern Nubia, flooding ancient ruins that had never been studied. Egypt and Sudan asked archaeologists from around the world to study these ruins quickly. The two governments allowed archaeologists to take half of what they excavated (uncovered) to their home countries. In 1963 and 1964 people who lived in the area —some of whose families had lived there for centuries—were resettled in Egypt and Sudan. Their homes and the remaining ruins of ancient Nubia then disappeared under Lake Nasser.

29

Muslims, and it particularly angered the non-Muslim population. A Sudanese army commander—John Garang, from the Dinka people—deserted and established the Sudanese People's Liberation Army (SPLA) in 1983. Civil war in the southern states raged again. The SPLA launched guerrilla hit-and-run attacks on government posts and soon controlled most of the south.

Throughout his term as Sudan's leader, Nimeiri thwarted many coup attempts by military officers who opposed his rule. Even after disbanding opposition groups and reshuffling his cabinet to reduce its power to overthrow him, Nimeiri faced troubled times. Riots and civil war continued to plague the Nimeiri government.

The famine crisis in Sudan during the 1980s was far greater than any other food shortage in the country's history. Throughout the 1980s, this crisis, as well as the civil war, resulted in substantial food shortages. The United Nations (UN) estimated that the drought severely affected a total of 4.5 million people in Darfur, Kurdufan, and the Red Sea region.

In April 1985, after sixteen years of Nimeiri's rule, army officers overthrew the president. Escalating civil war in the south, Nimeiri's poor economic management, governmental corruption, and reactions to police repression contributed to the coup's success. The spark, however, was a riot triggered by a huge increase in bread prices, which Nimeiri announced only days before the coup.

Shortly after taking power, the coup's leaders announced a program to return to civilian rule within a year. In an orderly election in 1986, the conservative Umma Party won a majority of seats. It formed a coalition to share power with the Democratic Unionist Party. The coalition selected Umma Party leader Sadiq al-Mahdi (the great-grandson of the Mahdi who had defeated the British) as prime minister.

The new government faced Sudan's ongoing problems. The civil war continued, and towns under the control of the SPLA became scenes of fighting and starvation. Drought and conflicts in neighboring countries brought many refugees to Sudan, which was unable to feed them. Thousands of people died as troops stopped relief food from getting to the south. In addition, heavy rains in 1988 caused massive flooding in the north, leaving many more Sudanese homeless and without food.

Al-Bashir and Civil War

The government of Sadiq al-Mahdi was unable to solve these serious problems, and in June 1989, the army overthrew the civilian regime. Coup leader General Omar Hassan al-Bashir named himself prime minister, suspended the constitution, detained members of the former cabinet, and censored the press. Al-Bashir was supported by Islamists, people who wanted Islam to be the dominant political, legal, and social force in the country. The fundamentalist National Islamic Front (NIF), led by Hassan al-Turabi, held enormous unofficial power. With NIF encouragement, al-Bashir reintroduced full Islamic law in 1991 nationwide.

In the face of renewed Sharia, southern rebels split along ethnic group lines over whether to fight for an independent southern Sudan or to seek a united but secular (nonreligious) Sudan. Garang's SPLA, composed mainly of Dinka, wanted the south to stay united with the more economically developed north and to keep access to the Red Sea coast. Several other rebel groups fought for a separate, independent south. Both northern and southern forces used a "scorched earth" style. They burned villages, destroyed crops, and stole livestock. Hundreds of thousands of Sudan's refugees streamed north into Chad, Ethiopia, and other neighboring countries. Both rebel groups and the government sometimes prevented relief agencies from delivering food and medicine to refugee camps, increasing the suffering caused by violence, starvation, and disease.

In the 1990s, Sudan lost most of its regional support through its militaristic brand of Islamic politics and its many border disputes. Neighboring Eritrea, Ethiopia, Uganda, and Kenya formed a group to encourage Sudan to pursue peace. International support also dwindled with Sudan's support of terrorism, including the extremist Islamist

Many **Sudanese homes have been destroyed during civil war.** Both northern and southern groups burned and looted many villages like this one.

President Omar al-Bashir raises his hands during a military parade in 1995.

leader Osama bin Laden and his network al-Qaeda. Bin Laden lived in Khartoum from 1991 until 1996, when he moved to Afghanistan. He retained close ties to the Sudanese government after his move.

In 1996 al-Bashir was reelected president, and al-Turabi's NIF gained control of the parliament. In 1997 the government signed a cease-fire with some rebel group leaders. The terms of the agreement called for the right of self-determination for the south. But the government set no date for a referendum (public vote) to determine southern independence. The government also gave no sign that it would remove Sharia from the south. The war continued.

In August 1998, the United States launched missiles to destroy a pharmaceutical plant outside Khartoum. The U.S. government suspected the factory was part of a chemical weapons program linked to Osama bin Laden. Bin Laden was linked to the bombings of two U.S. embassies in East Africa earlier that year. The United States also imposed sanctions (economic restrictions) on Sudan.

In 1999 al-Bashir and al-Turabi ended their partnership when al-Turabi pushed for a law to reduce the president's power. In response, al-Bashir again suspended the constitution and dissolved the al-Turabi-controlled parliament. The following year, al-Bashir was reelected president in elections observers condemned as corrupt. Al-Bashir had al-Turabi arrested and imprisoned in 2001, and parliament began again. The government also launched major attacks on the Nuba people, a largely Muslim, black African people who live in the Nuba Mountains of central Sudan.

On September 11, 2001, extremist Islamist terrorist attacks—organized by Osama bin Laden's al-Qaeda network—struck the United States. Sudan's leaders cooperated with efforts against international terrorism after the strikes but objected to the presence of Western troops on Islamic holy lands. However, without the influence of radical Islamist al-Turabi, al-Bashir's government improved Sudan's strained international relations.

In 2002 the al-Bashir government of Sudan and the Garang-led SPLA engaged in peace talks in Machakos, Kenya. The talks led to the Machakos Protocol, a statement of intent to end the war. Peace talks continued in 2003, and the general situation in Sudan began to improve.

◉ Darfur and Peace

In 2003 violence surged again when a separate rebellion broke out in Darfur, an area in western Sudan that is almost the size of Texas. Darfur is wholly Muslim but contains more than thirty different ethnic groups, some Arab and some non-Arab. Competition over scarce resources—such as water and fertile land—had long challenged Darfur. The beginning of an oil industry in Darfur added to the tension.

Claiming to represent non-Arab Africans in Darfur, rebels protested decades of government neglect. They demanded full economic, political, and social rights for Darfur. They also wanted oil wealth from the region to be shared equally. To combat the rebels, the government armed local Arab militias. These groups are commonly called *janjaweed*, an Arabic term meaning "horse and gun." The loosely organized groups went far beyond ending the rebellion. Old rivalries between non-Arab farmers and Arab nomads resurfaced. The janjaweed attacked non-Arab civilians, often with government backup, including aerial bombing of villages. The rebel groups, often loosely organized and undisciplined, also sometimes killed and harassed civilians.

Darfur's total population of 6 million suffered heavily during the conflict. An estimated 100,000 lost their lives in the violence, and another 180,000 died from hunger and disease. The janjaweed drove 2 million villagers from their homes in "ethnic-cleansing" attacks that included rape and the destruction of homes, crops, and livestock. More than 200,000 people left their homes to find refuge across the border in Chad.

The conflict in Darfur has displaced almost 2 million people. These **refugees** are waiting in line for food. To learn more about Sudanese refugees, go to www.vgsbooks.com for links.

Meanwhile, peace talks concerning the civil war continued. On January 9, 2005, in Nairobi, Kenya, the government of Sudan and the Garang-led SPLA signed the Comprehensive Peace Agreement to end the war. The peace deal allows the south to vote in 2011 on whether or not to become independent.

In March 2005, the UN sent ten thousand military personnel to Sudan to coordinate with the African Union (AU) mission. The AU is an organization of African countries for political and social stability. The aim was to protect human rights in Darfur, support the peace treaty, help resettle displaced persons, and provide humanitarian aid. Hope is high that the settling of the civil war will eventually bring peace to the entire country. In July 2005, southern rebel leader John Garang became vice president of Sudan. Three weeks later, Garang died in a helicopter crash. Riots broke out around the country resulting in 130 deaths and fears that the peace process was threatened. But leaders on both sides vowed to continue the peace process with no changes. Garang's successor, Salva Kiir, became Sudan's new vice president and promised to fulfill Garang's vision of a peaceful Sudan.

◉ Government

An authoritarian military regime led by President al-Bashir has ruled Sudan since 1989. Al-Bashir served as a dictator, and all political parties were banned. In 1997 the regional structure of the country was replaced with the creation of twenty-six states. The central

Sudan's then vice president Ali Osman Mohamed Taha *(left)* and Sudanese People's Liberation Army leader John Garang *(right)* show the signed **peace accord** in Nairobi, Kenya, on January 9, 2005.

government, based in Khartoum, controls the states. A governor administers each state. The Sudanese legislature is called the National Assembly. Elections under al-Bashir were flawed, and al-Bashir often appointed members of parliament. The judicial system sought to impose Sharia as the law of the land, a major cause of the civil war between north and south.

With the 2005 Comprehensive Peace Agreement, the government of Sudan began a major restructuring. The agreement provides for the creation of a new constitution and new arrangements for power sharing and wealth sharing between the north and south.

In July 2005, the National Assembly approved an interim constitution. A central point of the constitution states that Islamic law will not be applied in the south. The constitution also lays out freedom of religion and expression as human rights. John Garang of the SPLA became the vice president of Sudan. He and al-Bashir signed the new interim constitution. After Garang's death, fellow former rebel Salva Kiir became the vice president. New governmental institutions will be created by 2006, and a new, nationally united government will be installed. Democratic elections will be held by 2009. In 2011 the south will have a referendum to determine whether or not to secede.

Visit www.vgsbooks.com for links to websites with up-to-date information about the political and humanitarian struggles in Sudan.

THE PEOPLE

The 39.1 million inhabitants of Sudan belong to many ethnic groups. Accurate census counts are not available due to Sudan's unstable conditions. Black African groups make up 52 percent of the population. These groups mostly live in the southern third of Sudan. Arabs make up 40 percent of the population, mostly living in the northern two-thirds of the country. About 6 percent of the population are Beja people, who have lived in the Red Sea Hills region for at least five thousand years. People from other countries compose about 2 percent of the population.

With a young population—about 45 percent of the citizenry is younger than 15 years old—Sudan's population is expected to keep growing. The average number of children a woman will have in her lifetime is 5.4. The projected population for the year 2050 is 84.2 million people.

Population density averages 40 people per square mile (15 per sq. km). Rural areas are home to 70 percent of Sudan's people. Urban people mostly live in Khartoum.

Ethnic Groups

Most black Africans in the south are part of the Nilotic ethnic group. Nilotic groups are mostly non-Muslims. The largest Nilotic group is the Dinka, with more than 1 million people. They speak a language also called Dinka. Most Dinka traditionally herd cattle near the White Nile. During the rainy season, they live in permanent settlements and grow crops such as millet and pumpkins. Cattle provide almost every other useful thing: milk for food, butter for oiling the skin and cooking, urine for dyeing hair and tanning hides, and dung for fuel. Hides are used for mats, drums, cloth, and rope. Horns and bones are carved into tools and musical instruments. Dinka art, music, dance, and religion reflects the importance of cattle. Some Dinka are Christians, but most practice a traditional religion with many divine powers.

The Nuer, with about 300,000 people, and the Shilluk, with roughly 120,000 people, are other important Nilotic groups. The cattle-herding

This is a group of **Dinka dancers** in southern Sudan. Dance is considered an important form of expression for many Sudanese ethnic groups.

Nuer are closely related to the Dinka. The two are traditional rivals who engage in mutual cattle raiding. During the civil war, they sometimes fought each other as well as the northern government for dominance. Living along the White Nile, the Shilluk are herders, farmers, and skillful fishers with nets and spears. In the past, they also hunted hippopotamuses until these river animals became a protected species.

The Fur are black Africans who are Muslims but not Arabs. Having settled in the area around the Marra Mountains long ago, the Fur composed an independent Islamic sultanate until they were absorbed by other powers. Mostly farmers, the Fur have ethnic ties to groups in neighboring Chad. Darfur, the name of the region they live in, means "homeland of the Fur."

Nubians have their own language and maintain strong ethnic loyalties. However, Nubians also speak Arabic as a second language and are Muslims. Residents of the ancient land of Nubia, many Nubians had to resettle when the Aswan High Dam flooded their land in the mid-1960s. Many moved to work in Khartoum or Port Sudan. Some Nubians still inhabit the country's northernmost reaches.

Arabs are the most numerous people in northern and central Sudan. They speak Arabic and practice Islam. But Sudanese Arabs are split by many different regional and

ethnic loyalties and many different ways of life. The Arabic-speaking Juhayna are nomadic people, although some members have become more settled in recent times. The Jaali live along the banks of the Nile between Dunqulah and the area north of Khartoum.

Being Arab is not defined by race. Intermarriage, conquest, and migration have formed many different Arab racial compositions. Some Sudanese Arabs are descendants of Semitic (southwest Asian) peoples from the Arabian Peninsula. Others are descended from pre-Islamic indigenous, or native, people. For instance, some Arab nomads in Darfur are indigenous Bedouin people who are sometimes as dark-skinned as the black African Muslims with whom they are in conflict. Arabs follow different forms of Islam as well, and have different political loyalties. Though the Sudanese government is Islamist, not all Arabs or all Muslims support it or want Sharia to be the law of the land.

In the mid-twentieth century, six hundred ethnic groups speaking about four hundred languages made Sudan one of the world's most socially complex countries. But decades of war and drought deeply affected traditional ethnic societies. Faced with loss of livelihood or violently separated from family, people moved to cities for work, and their traditional ways of life were lost. Many small groups were absorbed into larger groups. The smallest ethnic groups, numbering a few hundred people, were even less resistant to the country's stresses. They have been entirely wiped out.

The Beja are traditionally a nomadic group with a reputation for being great warriors. In modern times, about 800,000 Beja people live in different groups, speaking different languages. One group, the Bisharin, are well-known camel breeders. The government has encouraged the mostly Muslim Beja to give up the nomadic life. Many have settled around Port Sudan and work in the busy commercial city. Some Beja have become cotton farmers.

Port Sudan, located on the Red Sea, is Sudan's main shipping center. Many people move to big cities like Port Sudan for work.

Foreigners form a small percentage of Sudan's population. A large percentage of them are from western Africa, mainly Nigeria. Approximately 150,000 refugees from neighboring countries strain Sudan's already limited resources.

Education and Language

Due to war, a generation of Sudan's children has grown up with little formal education. The government provides six years of primary school for Sudanese children, but the country suffers from a shortage of schools and teachers. In addition, more schools exist in urban, northern areas than in the country and the south, though most Sudanese live in rural areas. About 59 percent of children attend primary school, and about 21 percent attend secondary schools or technical schools.

Though schools in the south are lacking, the southern Sudanese highly value education. Even in refugee camps, teachers do what they can with limited materials to educate the children. Learning

SCHOOL UNDER THE TREES

In her book, *The Lost Boys of Natinga: A School for Sudan's Young Refugees*, American journalist Judy Walgren describes life in a southern Sudanese refugee camp for children. She tells of meeting Gabriel, a young student in the school that meets outside in the shade of the trees:

"Sitting on the front pew is Gabriel Deng, a thin boy dressed in tattered clothes. Gaping wounds run up and down his legs. Gabriel says [a] prayer in the Dinka language....
'Please deliver your young generation from this suffering. Father, please deliver us from the war situation we are living in.'

"Gabriel tells me: 'When the war is finished, life will be good. When the war stops, the children will be able to learn in a proper place, in a real school, with books and classrooms.'"

Sudanese **schoolchildren** have their lessons under the shade of a fig tree, sitting on makeshift benches.

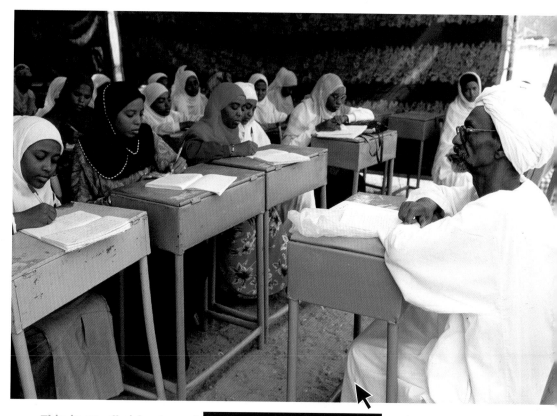

This is an all-girls class at **Omdurman Islamic University,** located near Khartoum. To learn more about the colleges of Sudan, visit www.vgsbooks.com for links.

English is considered very important, as teachers believe the students will need to communicate with people from the West to succeed in the future. Learning a common language is also important in a country with so many different languages. Many southerners speak Arabic and the language of their ethnic group. In 2005 a new school curriculum was developed for southern Sudan.

Fewer girls than boys attend school. Sudan's literacy rate—the percentage of people able to read and write a basic sentence—is 61 percent. Literacy is 72 percent for men and 50 percent for women.

Most of the institutions of higher learning, including the University of Khartoum and the Ahfad University for Women, are in the north. Not enough people have the education needed for skilled work. Sudan has lost many of its educated people to emigration.

Sudan's languages—estimated to number about one hundred— reflect the country's diversity. Arabic is the official language of Sudan and is spoken by all Arabs. Almost every group in Sudan uses Arabic as a first or second language. Arabic exists in many dialects, or variations. One form of spoken Arabic—called modern standard Arabic—is used in television and movies and among people who can't understand one another's dialect.

Because of British colonization and early missionary education, many Sudanese speak English. This international language serves unofficially as Sudan's second language.

Ethnic groups in Sudan speak a wide range of languages. Many of them, including the Dinka, Nuer, and Shilluk languages, are part of the Nilo-Saharan family of languages.

Clothing

In Sudan's cities, people usually wear Western clothing, although traditional dress is also common. Islam dictates that women—and men—dress modestly. Many Muslim women wear a sheetlike outer garment called a *toab* that covers their heads and reaches to their feet when they go out in public. Men may wear a long, loose robe, called a *jallabiyah*, along with either a small cap or a turban. Often these clothes are white, to reflect the hot sun. In rural areas, however (especially where the temperature is very hot), people do not wear much clothing. A pair of shorts or a lightweight dress is common dress in these places.

These girls wearing **lightweight dresses** are carrying water.

Hundreds of thousands of Sudanese people live in **refugee camps.** With Sudan's limited resources, it is difficult to meet the health-care needs of the people.

Health

Sudan does not have a well-developed health-care system. Medicine, medical supplies, and medical staff are often unavailable. Rural clinics and hospitals are few. Life expectancy in Sudan is 57 years, and the infant mortality rate is 69 deaths for every 1,000 live births. The rate of children who die before they reach the age of 5 is 127 out of every 1,000. Though far worse than Western figures, these statistics are about average for African countries.

As with every other area of life in Sudan, war, ethnic violence, and poor environmental conditions cause far-reaching problems in the population's health. Yellow fever, malaria, cholera, tuberculosis, and dysentery especially afflict Sudan's low-income groups. The rate of HIV/AIDS is 2.3 percent, which means about half a million Sudanese have the deadly disease. The rate is increasing.

Visit www.vgsbooks.com for links to websites with additional information about the people of Sudan, including the cultural traditions of different tribes as well as health-care and humanitarian concerns that affect the entire country.

About half of all Sudanese have access to safe drinking water, a situation that further complicates health care. Waterborne parasites are common. Guinea worm, for instance, is a parasite that enters the body through drinking water. It grows up to several feet long and causes blisters, boils, and tumors. The worm can be avoided by pouring water through a filter. Another parasite causes river blindness. A pill prevents this disease. But war-and-poverty affected regions so there is a lack of even simple medicines, such as aspirin. Basic health education is needed to address these challenges.

Malnutrition is a major problem in Sudan, making people more vulnerable to diseases. In Darfur health experts warn that malnutrition and death rates among displaced people are likely to increase. Crowded conditions in refugee camps increase the rapid spread of infectious diseases. Refugees depend on aid to survive. In the rainy season, roads are impassable, and food and medicines cannot reach the camps. Rebel groups sometimes attack aid workers and impede the delivery of supplies.

Sudan has the highest rate of female genital mutilation (FGM) in the world. In this traditional practice, up to 90 percent of girls in the north have their external genitalia cut away and the vagina sewed almost totally closed. In rural areas, FGM may be performed with nonsterile instruments and without anesthetics for the pain or antibiotics for infection. FGM can result in infections, ongoing pain, difficulties in childbirth, and death. The Sudanese government has said it is committed to ending FGM.

THE RULE OF THE DESERT

When he traveled through northern Sudan, travel writer Paul Theroux was impressed to see the way people help each other in the harsh desert land. He describes one such instance, when he and Ramadan, his driver, came across a car with a tire that had exploded in the heat:

"Three men stood by the old car in the hot bright desert, the only features in the landscape. Ramadan conferred with them and the men explained their dilemma, which was obvious: a blowout, no spare tire, no traffic on the road; they needed a new tire. They got into our truck and we drove them about fifty miles and dropped them off at a repair shop in a small town way off the road. The lengthy detour of an hour and a half was considered normal courtesy, like the rule of the sea that necessitates one ship helping another in trouble, no matter what the inconvenience. And here the desert much resembled a wide sea."

—Paul Theroux,
Dark Star Safari: Overland from Cairo to Cape Town

Family Life and Women

War has greatly affected family patterns, especially in the south, where families have been torn apart. Traditionally, the family is the center of Sudanese life. Extended families meet the social, economic, and emotional needs of all related members. For instance, if children are orphaned, relatives take them in. Families are responsible for the old, sick, and the mentally ill. Elders are respected, and children are well loved but expected to be obedient. Among many ethnic groups, clans form the main political unit.

Marriage in Sudan is a union between families, not just between two people. Arranged marriages are common among Muslims. Young people of non-Arab groups may choose their own partners. Bridewealth, or the giving of a dowry, is a widespread custom. The groom gives bridewealth to the bride's family as compensation for the family's loss. Cattle are the main form of bridewealth.

Women are the main caretakers of the family. Usually girls and women stay in the home and care for the household. Women in rural areas grow crops and haul water and firewood. Men dominate political life, while women tend to have more power in the home. Southern women have greater freedoms than northern Arab Muslim women. Southern women are more likely to have a voice in public affairs. Women from liberal, educated, and wealthier families have greater access to education and jobs.

THE GRASS SUFFERS

An African saying relates "When two elephants fight, the grass suffers." In Sudan women and children have been like the grass caught under fighting groups. Women and girls suffer the most from lack of education, food, and health care, and are more likely to be victims of sexual abuse. Women and children make up the vast majority of refugees. Yet women have almost no voice in political decision making, with only two female ministers in parliament. Women activists are demanding more involvement in the peace-building process and the furture government of Sudan.

CULTURAL LIFE

Sudan's cultural life is complex and shaped by geography, history, and religion. Religion is a very important part of the culture, and many Sudanese are deeply religious. Islam and the Arab cultures of North Africa are the dominant cultural forces in the north. The south has myriad traditions practiced by individual groups.

▷ Religion

Islam is Sudan's main religion, with followers among almost all the ethnic groups in the country. Muslims make up about 70 percent of the total Sudanese population. Non-Muslims mostly inhabit southern Sudan. About 25 percent practice traditional African beliefs, and 5 percent are Christian. Many people who follow Islam or Christianity blend ancient traditional beliefs with the non-African religions. The combination of different forms of spiritual beliefs or practices is called syncretism.

Islam has many different forms, but they all share five main principles, or the five pillars of Islam. Belief in one god (Allah) and

Muhammad as his prophet is the central pillar. The other four are prayer five times daily, regular almsgiving (charity), fasting during the holy month of Ramadan, and making a pilgrimage to the holy city of Mecca if possible. *Islam* means "submission" in Arabic and comes from the word for "peace." *Muslim* means "one who submits," and the Quran, Islam's holy book, teaches that an individual should submit to a code of conduct based on honesty, faithfulness, and tolerance.

Sudanese Muslims are mostly of the Sunni—or traditional—sect, which features strong Islamic brotherhoods. These religious orders are influential in many African nations and make demands—sometimes including political support—on their followers.

People whose ancestors originated in southern Sudan often practice traditional African religions. The central belief in traditional religions is that the spirit of life, or consciousness, resides in all things, including people, animals, plants, the earth, and natural forces such as weather. Keeping the circle of life in balance is very important. The

A Shilluk Creation Myth

Different people have different stories about the way the earth and living creatures came to be. The Shilluk, who are Nilotic farmers and fishers, tell a story about how Juok, the supreme god, created people. Juok declared, "I will give human beings long legs so that they can be like flamingos who stride through the shallow waters while fishing. And I will give them long arms so they can swing their farming tools the way monkeys swing sticks. I will give people mouths to eat with and eyes so they can see their food. I will give them tongues to sing with. And I will give them ears to hear their songs."

tradition teaches that powerful ancestors who have died are spiritually alive. Spiritual healers hold rituals to contact the ancestor spirits, either to ask for help or healing or to combat evil spirits. Rituals and specific beliefs vary greatly from group to group.

◉ Literature

Written classical Arabic is the language of the Quran, which is the most important book for many Sudanese Muslims. Besides reading and studying the Quran, Sudanese Muslims also tell a wealth of stories about the saints of Islam, or the holy men and women who were closest to Allah.

Contemporary Sudanese Arab literature—including poetry, short stories, and novels—is well known throughout Arab countries. Little is translated into English, however.

Government censorship has limited freedom of speech in Sudan. It is difficult for Arab writers to get published if they express disagreement with the government's point of view.

Many Sudanese writers live outside Sudan. Tayeb Salih is Sudan's most popular writer, but he has spent most of his adult life living abroad. Two of his novels—*The Wedding of Zein* and *The Season of the Migration to the North*—have been translated into English. His themes are often political, examining the role of women and men and the relations between the West and the Arab world. Leila Aboulela lives in Scotland. Her first novel, *The Translator* (1999), is about the conflicts of a young Sudanese woman living in exile. Aboulela won the Caine Prize for African Writing in 2000 for her short story "The Museum."

Raouf Musad is a playwright, journalist, and novelist from northern Sudan who lives in Holland. His Christian background is an important part of his basic themes of identity and belonging. Musad has published many books, including the novel *Ostrich Egg* in 1994. In 2004 he started a small publishing company with other Arab writers living outside the Arab world.

Southern Sudanese have a highly developed storytelling culture that passes on history and beliefs from generation to generation. Traditional stories, or myths, include themes such as the way the world was created and the history of ancestors. Mythical heroes, animals, and gods often figure in the stories. This oral literary culture has partially been lost due to war, migration, and modernization.

Because of a history of cultural oppression and lack of formal education, few southern Sudanese are published authors. This is starting to change. In 2003 two young southern Sudanese living abroad published accounts of their experiences as slaves in Sudan and of how they escaped. Francis Bok, a Christian Dinka, wrote *Escape from Slavery*, relating how Arab raiders captured him when he was seven. Mende Nazer, a black African Muslim from the Nuba Mountains, tells her story in *Slave: My True Story*. She, too, was captured as a child by Arab slavers and forced to work for years as a slave servant. Both write about the traditions of their people as well as the horrors of slavery. *They Poured Fire on Us from the Sky*, published in 2005, is a record of war seen from the point of view of children. The authors, Benson Deng, Alephonsion Deng, and Benjamin Ajak, are three young Dinka men who live in the United States.

MODERN SLAVERY IN SUDAN

Slavery in Sudan is not a thing of the past. International human rights groups accuse Sudanese Arab militias of kidnapping black Africans, especially women and children, to take north and sell as slaves. Reports also indicate that southern troops forced boys into military service. The U.S. Bureau of African Affairs declares, "Slavery in Sudan is characterized by violent capture and abductions, subjection to forced labor with no pay, denial of a victim's freedom of movement and choice, prohibition of the use of native language, and the denial of contact with the victim's family." In the twenty-first century, the Arab word for "slave," *abd* (pronounced "abeed"), remains in use to refer to southerners.

Art

Islam is the primary historic influence on artistic expression in northern Sudan. Calligraphy, or decorative writing, is Islam's most beautiful art. It is used in writing beautiful copies of the Quran by hand. Ornate calligraphic verses from the Quran also decorate buildings and objects such as vases.

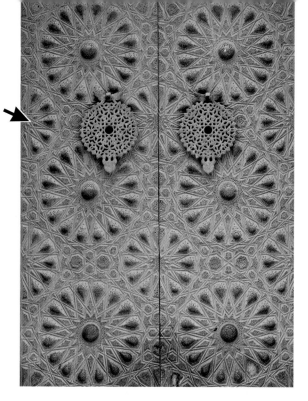

These bronze doors are from fourteenth century Sudan. **Islamic art** is still used to decorate important buildings such as mosques.

Islam discourages images of humans, so Islamic art has developed intricate geometric patterns into a high art. Some of these patterns are based on complicated mathematical formulas. The patterns may incorporate natural elements such as flowers and animals. These graceful designs are found on tiles, carpets, and pottery, and in calligraphy.

Hassan Musa is a modern calligrapher and illustrator who creates books of Sufi (a branch of Islamic mysticism) and other Sudanese folktales for children and adults. Kamala Ibrahim Ishaq is a painter who lives in Omdurman. Her expressive modern art was part of an international exhibit titled "Breaking the Veils, Women Artists from the Islamic World." The art of fifty women from twenty-two Islamic countries was displayed in this traveling exhibit from 2002 to 2004, organized by Queen Noor of Jordan.

A famous hadith (Islamic saying) declares, "Allah is beautiful and loves beauty."

Modern artists in Sudan have not always been free to express themselves if their art displeased the Islamist government. Some Sudanese Arab artists live and exhibit their art abroad.

Many non-Arab ethnic groups practice body art—adorning the human body and hair. In an environment with few resources, people use whatever is at hand to express themselves, to announce group identity, and to create beauty. The Dinka, especially young people, use their bodies as canvases to paint patterns and designs. They use paint made from ash or cattle dung. Nilotic peoples shave or sculpt their hair into designs set in place with dung or mud.

Hair may be dyed a dark orange color with cattle urine. Beads or feathers may be woven into the hair. Some groups also create permanent designs on their bodies in a process called scarification (tattoos made with scars).

The Nuba people are famous for their elaborate body art. Designs on the body are beautiful, but they also have social meanings, indicating age, marital and social status, and group identity. Skin anointed with oil and pigment glows with ochre (reddish brown or yellow clay). Nuba wrestlers cover themselves in wood ash, which is considered to have the sacred power and strength of the tree it came from. Hairstyles are elaborate and may take hours to create. Nuba scarification begins in childhood, with the shallow cutting of skin in patterns. Ash is rubbed into the cuts to form raised scars. Patterns decorating the body are rich in symbolism. This personal art form is being lost due to years of civil war, which has disrupted or destroyed cultural practices.

In a climate where it is often too hot to wear many clothes, beaded clothing and jewelry are artistic fashion statements. People may also weave beads into hair. Unmarried Dinka women traditionally wore beaded garments draped around their necks and shoulders.

A Sudanese woman wears colorful beads in her hair and as necklaces.

These garments were made of thousands of tiny beads strung into a kind of very wide necklace. Dinka men wore a kind of beaded corset. Western-style clothes have replaced these beaded clothes for everyday use, but people still wear them for special occasions.

Handicrafts throughout the country are made of ivory, shells, and wood, including black ebony. Decorative leather items, needlework, and beaded jewelry are also common. The southern Sudanese are known for their carved wooden figures. In the eastern and western deserts of Sudan, craftspeople make swords and spears. The silver-smiths, ivory carvers, and leatherworkers of Omdurman are famous.

Everyday objects, such as calabashes (gourd utensils) or wooden stools, are often decorated with designs. Women make brightly colored baskets with geometric designs. Clay vessels are usually made by women too. They build up coils of clay into the correct shape for cooking or carrying water. Using colored minerals and sharp tools, the potters add color and patterns to the clay. The pot is fired (baked hard) in a hole in the ground that is covered with burning straw and dung.

A **nomadic man** sews colorful dresses in Kassala.

◉ Music and Dance

Sudanese music is rich and unique, with deep roots. Nubian singers have been famous for their musical skills for thousands of years. Drums and clapping accompanied the complicated rhythms and chants of ancient Nubia. Incorporating sounds from eastern and western African cultures, as well as Roman, Arab, and Turkish musical styles over the centuries, modern Nubian music has a distinctive beat and force.

Islam does not forbid music and dance, but the ruling Islamic party has outlawed public performances that they consider immoral. Sufis—Muslims who follow a mystical form of Islam—use music as part of their religious observances, unlike most other Muslims. Mysticism is the spiritual effort of an individual to come into direct contact with Allah. Sufis hold devotional rituals in which they dance and spin until they enter a kind of religious trance. They also chant as a religious activity, bringing focus to the deep meaning within the words. On Fridays, the Muslim holy day, people come to watch Sufis in Khartoum celebrate their rituals of music and movement.

Sufi Muslim gospel music in Sudan—called *madeeh* (meaning "praise" in Arabic)—is sung to celebrate the prophet Muhammad. It has little or no musical accompaniment. The lead chanters tap a rhythm as the people gathered sing along, swaying to the sound.

Madeeh is the foundation of *haqibah,* the root of modern northern Sudanese music. This style is a blend of voices accompanied by percussion instruments, including small hand drums called *tabla* and the tambourine-like *riq.* Occasionally the *qanum* (a stringed instrument) or the *oud,* an Arabian lute, is used for melody. Northern Sudanese music in the twentieth century changed with the introduction of instruments from both the East and West, including violin, accordion, guitars, and brass instruments.

Different ethnic groups each have their own musical traditions, which include dance. People have songs for every type of work, such as planting and harvesting, fishing and carrying water. Singing and dancing usually accompany religious and social events. Drums are central to southern Sudanese music and dance. Another common instrument is the lyre, made with metal strings. The music of the Dinka of southern Sudan reflects the central role cattle play in their lives. A young man traditionally receives an ox as part of a ritual initiating him into manhood. The man often composes songs in praise of his ox. These special cattle are known as song oxen. Lyrics in songs throughout Sudan often send powerful political messages too. The loss of homelands to the Aswan High Dam is a common Nubian musical lament.

> Nubian music has an impressive ancestry. In the fifteenth century collection *Stories of One Thousand and One Nights*, or *Arabian Nights*, reputedly told by Queen Shahrazad of Arabia, it is recorded that "on entering Paradise, you will hear the sound of nightingales and Nubian singers. . . ."

Sports, Recreation, and Holidays

Soccer is Sudan's most popular sport. Basketball and volleyball are very popular too. Camel and horse racing are traditional competitions. Men also participate in running, swimming, boxing, and traditional fighting. Young Dinka and other tribal men engage in sparring matches—mock battles with shields and sticks. These bouts honed fighting skills and demonstrated a man's ability to protect his home and family from cattle raiders.

Similarly, wrestling is a popular sport among the people of the Nuba Mountains. At harvesttime, people from different villages gather to celebrate and to watch trained young men compete in wrestling matches. The wrestlers adorn their bodies with wood ash in geometric designs and wear headdresses of wood, cloth, animal skins, and feathers, in the style of warriors. Drumming, foot pounding, and chanting accompany the fierce outdoor matches, which end when one man pins his opponent's shoulders to the ground. At the end of a day of matches, one wrestler is declared champion. The day ends in feasting. Children often play at pretend wrestling matches.

Soccer is Sudan's most popular sport. These boys play **soccer** with a rag ball.

Children play with locally available materials and enjoy games such as hide-and-seek. *Anyok* is a popular game in southern Sudan. Two teams play with pointed spearlike sticks and one gourd. The object of the game is to spear the gourd when one team rolls it past the other team. Nuba children also play *kak*, a game with stones. Two players make a row of eight marble-sized pebbles. The first player, using just one hand, throws a stone up in the air, grabs one pebble off the ground, and catches the falling stone before it lands. If the stone hits the ground, it's the next player's turn. On the second round, the player has to pick up two pebbles before the stone lands, then three, then four, and so on.

In the north, Muslim women are forbidden to play any sport in the presence of men. Women are not so restricted in the south, but in general, Sudanese women do not play sports. They usually socialize in the home separate from the men. In the cities, men gather to socialize in coffee shops or in places where they smoke flavored tobacco in large water pipes.

Sudan commemorates its 1956 independence with a holiday, Independence Day, on January 1. Unity Day is March 3, and Labor Day is May 1. Practicing Muslims observe the holy month of Ramadan by fasting from all food and drink from sunup till sundown. The feast of Eid al-Fitr marks the end of Ramadan. Islamic holy days follow a lunar calendar. In the south, both Christians and traditionalists celebrate

IBM

Sudanese life and bureaucracy proceeds at a relaxed pace. A Sudanese joke states that IBM runs the country. This refers not to the computer company but to the frequently heard Arabic words *inshallah*, *bokra*, and *malesh*. *Inshallah* means "if God wills it" and is used to express that something may happen . . . or it may not—only God knows. *Bokra* means "tomorrow." It is used to mean some unknown time in the future when something may happen . . . maybe. *Malesh* means "sorry." People use it often to express regret because many things—such as buses or office work—do not run on time or efficiently in Sudan.

Christmas on December 25. Rural people celebrate important events, such as harvesttime, with music, dance, and feasting.

◎ Food

Sudanese cuisine is fairly simple. Millet, sorghum, and corn are staple foods, or the main sources of nutrition. They are boiled, ground into flour for bread, or prepared as porridge. Highly seasoned soups and stews may accompany them. Cooks make the stews from herbs and vegetables, such as onions, pumpkins, eggplant, and okra, to which they sometimes add eggs or meat, if available.

When meat is available, Sudanese eat beef, chicken, goat, and mutton (meat of a sheep) or lamb. Chunks of roasted meat on a spit are called shish kebabs. *Shwarma* is freshly sliced strips of roasted meat. Along rivers, people eat fish. For practicing Muslims, all meat must be halal, or holy to eat. Islam forbids the eating of pork. Cattle herders eat a lot of milk and dairy products, such as cheese and yogurt.

A common meal in northern Sudan features *ful*, or fava beans cooked in oil. *Taamiya*, or falafel, are balls of fried, ground chickpeas and spices. *Fatta*, a dish of peas, lentils, tomatoes, and cheese with bread, is another common meal. The nomads of the northern deserts live mainly on milk and dairy products from camels and goats. These animals are too valuable to be killed and eaten, except on special occasions. Desert animals such as rabbits or antelope occasionally add meat to the diet.

The southern Sudanese make soups with vegetables, including cassava (a starchy root, also called manioc) or sweet potatoes. Peanuts are boiled or added to stews. Fresh fruits in areas where there is plenty of rain include bananas, melons, mangoes, and pineapple. The seed pod of the tamarind tree provides an acidy-sweet pulp that is pressed and used as flavoring in foods or made into a drink.

MILLET BREAKFAST PORRIDGE

Sudanese eat meals twice a day, in the morning and evening. Many Sudanese people eat millet in some form at every meal. It may be served sweetened with dates at breakfast or with a spicy stew in the evening. Herders eat it with milk. However, if there is nothing else to eat, millet alone may be the entire meal. This recipe for breakfast millet has been served over centuries, as far back as the ancient Nubians. You could try serving it with goat milk, available in health food stores.

2 cups water

⅛ teaspoon salt

½ cup millet

4 dates

1 cup milk (cow or goat)

1. Put water and salt in a saucepan and bring to a boil over high heat.
2. Add millet to boiling water and stir briefly. Turn heat to low, cover the pot, and set a timer for 25 minutes.
3. Remove pits from dates, if necessary. Chop dates into small pieces. Add dates to cooking millet. Continue cooking, stirring occasionally so the porridge doesn't stick to the pot.
4. After 25 minutes, serve hot porridge in bowls. Pour milk over each serving.

Serves 4

Tea is the most popular beverage, served very sweet and sometimes milky, spiced, or mixed with mint. Turkish coffee (hot, sweet, thick, and black) is also common, and *jebana* is sweet coffee spiced with ginger, cardamom, or cinnamon. Islamic law forbids alcoholic beverages everywhere in Sudan. However, southerners customarily drink beer called *marisa* made from sorghum. Fruit juices, including mango, lemon, watermelon, and banana juice, make refreshing drinks. Dried karkaday, flowers from a kind of hibiscus, are made into a deep red tea that is served cold.

Visit www.vgsbooks.com for links to websites with additional information about Sudan's literature, music, dance, cuisine, and more.

THE ECONOMY

Sudan is largely a poor, agricultural society. Much of the population lives at or below the poverty line. The World Bank estimates that the per capita income (total national income averaged per person) is less than $400 a year. War and drought have devastated the southern economy and used up half of the government's annual budget. Unemployment is close to 19 percent. Sudan's entire foreign debt is equal to the total amount of goods produced by the nation each year.

With the start of significant oil production in 1999, Sudan's economy took an upswing. The government also began large economic changes recommended by the International Monetary Fund (IMF, a UN financial agency). These reforms included currency changes and ongoing privatization, or selling government-owned companies to private investors.

Beginning after the peace talks of 2002, Sudan's central government started to repair its economic relations with the south. North and

south reached an agreement on several major economic issues, including how to share oil revenues fairly. Sudan still faces major economic challenges due to its limited and damaged infrastructure (the public works that help a country run), such as roads, waterworks, the electricity grid, and communication systems.

Sudan has good natural resources. The Nile is a source of water, fertile soil, hydropower, and transportation. The seacoast gives the country access to trade. Minerals are present in good supply, and the country has enough oil for its needs. Sudan's people want peace, prosperity, and education. Peace between north and south offers the possibility to use these resources to build a healthy economy, especially through educating the children. But conflict in Darfur continues to destabilize the economy. A 2005 UN plan pledged $4.5 billion in aid to Sudan to help the country rebuild. The United States is the largest contributor. But the aid depends on Sudan's government bringing about a peaceful settlement of the Darfur situation.

A worker gathers **cotton** near a field. Cotton is Sudan's most important crop. To learn more about agriculture in Sudan, visit www.vgsbooks.com for links.

Agriculture

Agriculture, including forestry and fishing, accounts for 39 percent of the country's GDP (gross domestic product, or the value of goods and services produced in a country each year). About 80 percent of Sudan's people are engaged in agriculture. Nearly all of them live as subsistence farmers, only able to produce food for themselves and their families. In the central part of the country along the Nile, farm machinery helps to produce food for export. Subsistence farmers rely on traditional methods of working the soil.

GUM ARABIC

The candy you eat or the gum you chew may have an ingredient from Sudan. Sudan is the world's leading exporter of gum arabic, a substance that oozes from certain acacia trees (*Acacia arabica*). Workers collect the solid, walnut-sized gum from the trees by hand. Gum arabic is used in the manufacture of ink, adhesives, medicine, and food thickeners, such as those found in chewing gum and candies.

The chief crops grown for food are millet, peanuts, sorghum, wheat, cassava, mangoes, bananas, and sweet potatoes. Cotton is Sudan's major cash crop, grown for export sales. Sudan also exports sugar and supplies 80 percent of the world's gum arabic, from acacia trees. Sesame is grown for vegetable oil used domestically and exported.

Covering 1.1 million acres (445,154 hectares), a government-owned farm in the fertile Gezira region is one of the largest irrigation projects in the world. Cotton is the main cash crop of this farming scheme. Millet, sorghum, and rice are also grown here for local consumption. Peanuts grow well in Gezira's heavy clay soil.

Sudanese farmers use a cultivation system called *harig*. They let native grasses (harig) spread until the grasses form a dense mat over the land. Then, after the early rains have nourished weed seeds under the mat, a dry spell allows farmers to burn off all the grass and weeds. This process leaves the land fertilized and ready for planting.

Raising livestock is a major activity of the Sudanese population. Herds graze throughout the countryside, except in the extremely dry areas of the north and in the southern regions, where disease-carrying tsetse flies cause illness and death among livestock. In the south, agriculture is mainly pastoral, and Sudanese herders chiefly tend cattle—mostly in a traditional rural setting. Farmers also raise sheep, goats, chickens, and camels. Sudan is a major supplier of sheep meat to the huge market of the Arab world.

Drought and desertification affect Sudan's food production. Parts of Sudan located in the Sahel, along the edge of the Sahara, suffer from long periods of little rainfall. Drought has hit this area frequently since the mid-1960s. In irrigated areas of the eastern and central regions of Sudan, low rainfall has also reduced

Rural African women traditionally plant crops while men tend the livestock. A study by the World Bank (a UN financial agency) found that if women received the same education as men, farm yields would increase by about 22 percent. Yet women receive only 5 percent of the agricultural technical training that the UN and other agencies provide.

An Arab Sudanese boy shepherds **sheep and goats** through parched grass.

crop production. Furthermore, violence in Darfur affects food production. Farming has become too dangerous to practice in areas affected by war, and mass starvation continues to plague the region.

Forestry and Fishing

Farmers have cleared large areas of Sudan's forests for agricultural use. Lacking other sources, people cut down forests for fuel. These processes have contributed to the expansion of the desert in semiarid regions that lie between true desert and wooded areas. Nevertheless, southern Sudan still has extensive forested lands, where hardwoods thrive. One of the main forest products is mahogany timber, a beautiful wood used for making furniture. The government has authorized the development of plantations for teak and oak in an effort to replenish the dwindling forests. Eucalyptus trees planted in irrigated agricultural areas help protect the soil from erosion and supply wood as fuel to local residents.

Sudan's fishing industry centers on the Nile River system. The industry has also developed fishing along the coast of the Red Sea and in lakes created by dams. Although Sudan has great potential for a thriving fish industry, most catches have fallen below anticipated levels. Moreover, rather than becoming sources of export income, fish hauls are needed locally as food.

Industry and Trade

Industry, including mining and manufacturing, employs 7 percent of the population and comprises 20 percent of the GDP. Oil is Sudan's most important industry. Substantial finds of petroleum were uncovered in the south and in Darfur in the 1970s. Civil war prevented development of this resource until 1991. In 1999 Sudan began exporting crude oil. This helped stabilize the economy. The central government received most of the oil wealth, however, and this increased regional ethnic tensions. The government has also been accused of forcibly displacing civilians who are in the way of oil fields. Sudan does not have enough oil to become an oil-wealthy country, but it does have enough to meet its own domestic energy and fuel needs, thus saving money that used to be spent on importing oil. The growing industry also attracts foreign investors to the country.

Sudan's other mineral deposits include chromite, mica (a thin, transparent metal), marble, and gypsum (a mineral used in making plaster). Chromite is produced largely in the Ingessana Hills. Mica exists in northern states, and gypsum is found along the coast of the Red Sea. New processing technologies attract foreign companies interested in gold and uranium deposits in the Red Sea Hills. The seabed off the Red Sea Coast is also rich in precious minerals, as well as copper, zinc, and iron. Sudan's mineral resources have not been fully developed.

Sudan's manufacturing sector is located in and around Khartoum. It focuses on light industries that use raw materials from the nation's agricultural output, such as cotton ginning (processing). Foodstuffs and textiles account for much of the manufactured products. Paper mills and sugar refineries are among Sudan's light industry base. Other factories turn out products such as cement, soap, pharmaceuticals, beverages, and shoes. Sudan's industrial workers also produce armaments and assemble automobiles and light trucks.

Historically, agriculture—especially cotton and livestock—accounted for most of Sudan's total export trade. In the twenty-first century, oil accounts for 70 percent of export earnings. Egypt, China, and Saudi Arabia are Sudan's major export partners. Sudan has traditionally spent far more on imports than it earns on exports, but in 2001, the oil industry changed that balance for the first time since independence. The country imports food, manufactured goods, transportation equipment, oil industry equipment (such as oil pipelines), medicines, and chemicals. Its major import partners are Saudi Arabia, China, Great Britain, Germany, India, and France.

◉ Energy

Wood and charcoal are the principal energy sources in Sudanese homes. Hydropower and oil fill the needs of industry. As Sudan's population has increased, the pressure on natural fuel sources, such as

Sudan uses dams to create electricity. This **dam** is on the Blue Nile.

wood, has also grown. Unregulated harvesting of Sudan's forests has resulted in soil erosion and shortages of fuel.

Sudan's electricity sector suffers from poor infrastructure linking people to power. Much of the country is not covered by an electrical grid and relies on small generators and wood for power. Power outages are frequent. Only 30 percent of the population, mostly urban, has access to electricity. The government is working to improve that percentage. The White Nile and Blue Nile are dammed at several places to generate hydroelectricity. Hydropower plants, such as the Rusayris Dam, supply electricity to urban centers in the north. Ten more dams are scheduled for completion in 2010.

Services, Transportation, and Communications

The service sector is comprised of jobs that provide services—such as education, tourism, and retail work—rather than goods. Sudan's service sector provides 41 percent of the GDP and employs 13 percent of the workforce, mostly in government. Tourism is very low as Sudan is the least visited country in Africa.

Two railways operate in Sudan. The British built the Sudan Railway in the late nineteenth century, linking central Sudan to Egypt and the Mediterranean Sea. The Gezira Light Railway connects Khartoum with the fertile cotton-growing regions of central Sudan. Although they need renovation, Sudan's 3,715 miles (5,978 km) of track are able to transport heavy freight and much agricultural produce.

Sudan has 7,394 miles (11,900 km) of roads. Only about one-third of them are paved. All-weather routes connect Port Sudan to Khartoum, and roads serve the oil fields of central and south Sudan. But most of the rest are little more than earthen tracks that are passable only in fair weather. Small amounts of freight—especially shipments that are needed quickly—travel by road in the dry season. International aid often has to be delivered by airlift. Sudan has sixty-three airports, twelve of which have paved runways.

Despite its many cataracts—which seriously inhibit navigation—the Nile River is a major inland transportation route for Sudan. Two reaches, or stretches of navigable waterway, exist. The reach in southern Sudan goes from Kusti to Juba, and the other reach extends between Kuraymah and Dunqulah. Equipment breakdowns, however, slow travel on both stretches of the waterway. Port Sudan is the country's main port. Oil pipelines run to the port's oil export terminal.

Sudan has about 1 million telephone lines and 650,000 mobile phones. The government is expanding the telephone system. A dozen radio stations and three television stations broadcast in the country.

The government owns and controls the media. People who can afford them use satellite dishes. Internet users number 300,000.

The Future

An Arab proverb maintains that Allah wept when he created Sudan. Another version of the proverb insists Allah laughed with delight when he created Sudan. Sudan's future is equally unknown. The 2005 peace agreement between the north and south holds hope for the future. But not all southern groups support the treaty, and cease-fires in Sudan have never been permanent in the past. The decade between 1972 and 1983 saw the only peace in Sudan since independence in 1956.

BETWEEN PEACE AND CONFLICT

In 2005 the UN secretary-general's special representative for Sudan, Jan Pronk, said, "Sudan stands poised between peace and conflict in 2005. The long-suffering people of the country have rarely faced a period of greater opportunity for peace in the last twenty years. The primary responsibility to realize this future lies with their leaders—who must not fail in this moment of truth."

Meanwhile, ethnic cleansing in Darfur continues. There are an estimated 2.2 million conflict-affected persons, including 1.6 million internally displaced persons, in the region. The numbers are expected to rise due to continued fighting and scarce resources.

The period of building peace is a fragile time. The United Nations in 2005 pledged $4.5 billion in humanitarian aid and to help the country reconstruct. Besides immediate food aid, Sudan needs assistance with health care, schools, economic development, law and civil service sectors, roads, sanitation, shelter, resettlement of refugees, protection of human rights, land-mine action, disarmament of rebel groups, and ethnic understanding.

The death of John Garang created new challenges for the peace process. Both northern and southern leaders urged the Sudanese people to keep Garang's vision of a peaceful, unified Sudan alive. At Garang's funeral on August 6, 2005, his successor, Salva Kiir, pledged, "As sure as day follows night, the torch he has kindled shall not be extinguished." The window of peace between north and south offers a time for the people of Sudan—and the international community—to address these challenges and move toward a lasting peace.

Timeline

CA. 6000 B.C. Humans settle in the Nubia region of northern Sudan.

CA. 2400 B.C. Kerma became the first kingdom in Cush, in northern Sudan.

1500 B.C. Egypt defeats and burns Kerma.

590 B.C. Egyptians force the Cushite kingdom centered in Napata to move its capital to Meroë.

24 B.C. Cushite ruler Candace (Queen) Amanirenas leads her army into battle and defeats Roman forces in Egypt.

A.D. 324 The armies of the Aksumite kingdom of northern Ethiopia defeat Meroë.

575 Following Egyptian, Ethiopian, and Roman influences, Nubia has become entirely Christian.

700s Arab armies bring Islam to northern Sudan. The Arabs arrange a series of treaties, or faqt, with the Nubian kingdoms.

CA. 1000 Nilotic ethnic groups migrate to the southwest of Sudan.

1300s Islamic soldiers called the Mamluks conquer the Nubian kingdom of Dunqulah.

1504 Funj sultans establish the first Muslim monarchy in Sudan, with its capital at Sennar.

CA. 1600 The Nubian form of Christianity has died out.

1820 An Egyptian army establishes Egyptian rule—called the Turkiya—in Sudan. The slave trade flourishes.

1885 Followers of the Mahdi, an Islamic reformer, attack and take Khartoum. British general Charles Gordon is killed in the attack. The Mahdi dies of fever.

1899 The Condominium Agreement establishes the joint authority of Britain and Egypt over Sudan. British rule ends the slave trade.

1920s British colonial irrigation programs transform large sections of central Sudan into productive farmland. Southern Sudan is not similarly developed.

1930 The British colonial government decrees that southerners are to regard themselves as ethnically distinct from northerners.

1956 Sudan formally becomes a self-governing republic on January 1. Southern groups rebel against the northern-led government's attempts to control them, starting a civil war.

1963 People who live in the Nubian area are resettled in Egypt and Sudan as their lands are flooded by the Aswan High Dam.

1969   Colonel Jaffar Nimeiri ends civilian rule when he assumes
       power in a coup.

1972   The Sudanese government agrees to give regional authority to the
       southern Sudanese. The civil war comes to a halt.

1980s Throughout the decade, famine in Sudan affects a total of 4.5 million
       people.

1982   Nimeiri imposes Sharia thoughout Sudan.

1983   John Garang forms the Sudanese People's Liberation Army (SPLA). Civil war
       starts again.

1984   Civil war in the south puts a stop to construction of the Jonglei Canal.

1985   Army officers overthrow Nimeiri.

1989   The army overthrows the civilian government of Sadiq al-Madhi. Coup leader General
       Omar Hassan al-Bashir declares himself prime minister and suspends the constitu-
       tion.

1991   Al-Bashir reintroduces full Islamic law. Osama bin Laden moves to Khartoum. Civil war
       rages on, devastating the economy and culture of Sudan.

1999   Sudan's economy takes an upswing with the beginning of significant oil exports. The
       dinar becomes Sudan's new currency.

2002   Al-Bashir's government and the SPLA engage in successful peace talks leading to the
       Machakos Protocol. Work of the artist Kamala Ibrahim Ishaq is part of an international
       exhibit titled "Breaking the Veils, Women Artists from the Islamic World."

2003   Peace talks between north and south continue, but violence surges in Darfur. The
       janjaweed engage in "ethnic cleansing" attacks, creating a humanitarian crisis. The
       government announces its commitment to ending female genital mutilation.

2005   The government of Sudan and the Garang-led SPLA sign the Comprehensive Peace
       Agreement, ending the civil war in the south. Garang becomes vice president in July,
       and he and al-Bashir sign an interim constitution. Genocide slows but continues in
       Darfur. Garang dies in a helicopter crash.

COUNTRY NAME Republic of the Sudan

AREA 967,500 square miles (2,505,825 sq. km)

MAIN LANDFORMS Dongotona Mountains, Didinga Hills, Imatong Mountains, Ironstone Plateau, Marra Mountains, Libyan Desert, Nuba Mountains, Nubian Desert, Red Sea Hills, Sahel, Sudd

HIGHEST POINT Mount Kinyeti, 10,456 feet (3,187 m) above sea level

LOWEST POINT Red Sea, sea level

MAJOR RIVERS Nile River, White Nile, Blue Nile, Sobat River, Atbara River

ANIMALS aardvarks, antelopes, buzzards, cranes, crocodiles, desert locusts, elephants, fennec foxes, gerbils, giraffes, herons, honey badgers, hyenas, ibex, jerboas, lions, monitor lizards, Nile perch, snakes, warthogs, wild sheep

CAPITAL CITY Khartoum

OTHER MAJOR CITIES Port Sudan, Kassala, Juba, Gedaref, Atbara, Dunqulah

OFFICIAL LANGUAGE Arabic

MONETARY UNITY Sudanese dinar (SDD). 1 dinar = 10 pounds.

CURRENCY

Sudanese dinar banknotes (paper money) come in denominations of 50, 100, 200, 500, 1,000 and 2,000. Coins are in the amounts of 5, 10, 20, and 50 dinar. However, the government only instituted the use of the dinar in 1999, and people commonly quote prices in Sudanese pounds. This can be confusing for visitors. One Sudanese dinar equals 10 pounds.

Currency Fast Facts

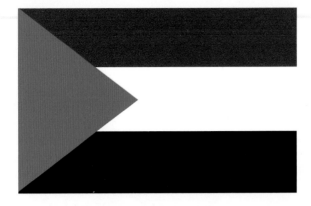

Sudan's flag was adopted in 1970. It has three horizontal stripes colored—in descending order—red, white, and black. A green triangle is on the hoist side (the side where the flag is attached to the pole). The colors have symbolic meaning. Green is the color of Islam and also stands for prosperity and agriculture; red stands for progress and the bloodshed in the struggle for independence; black refers to the meaning of the word *sudan* in Arabic and for the Mahdi-inspired revolution of the 1880s when a black flag was used; and white stands for peace and hope for the future.

Adopted at independence in 1956, the words of Sudan's national anthem were written by Sayed Ahmad Muhammad Salih and the music by Ahmad Murjan. These are the lyrics translated into English.

Nahnu Djundulla Djundulwatan
(We Are the Army of God and of Our Land)

We are the army of God and of our land,
We shall never fail when called to sacrifice.
Whether braving death, hardship or pain,
We give our lives as the price of glory.
May this our land, Sudan, live long,
Showing all nations the way.
Sons of the Sudan, summoned now to serve,
Shoulder the task of preserving our country.

 For a link to a site where you can listen to Sudan's national athem, "Nahnu Djundulla Djundulwatan," visit www.vgsbooks.com.

Flag

National Anthem

LEILA ABOULELA (b. 1964) Born in Khartoum, Aboulela learned English at school. She studied at the University of Khartoum and then the London School of Economics. In 1990 she moved to Scotland with her husband and their three children. Her first novel, *The Translator*, is about the conflicts of a young Sudanese widow living in Scotland. Aboulela won the Caine Prize for African Writing in 2000 for "The Museum," published in a short-story collection called *Opening Spaces.*

CANDACE (QUEEN) AMANIRENAS (ca. 40 B.C.–?) The ancient Nubian kingdom of Cush had a tradition of powerful queens called candaces. One of the most famous is Candace Amanirenas whose life is recorded in Roman history. The Nubians were constantly raiding their Roman-ruled Egyptian neighbors. In 24 B.C., on one of the raids, Amanirenas led her armies into battle and defeated the Romans. During battle she lost an eye. The Romans struck back, and Candace and her armies were defeated. Amanirenas was famous among the Romans for her courage and independence. The Roman governor Gaius Petronius called her One-Eyed Candace.

SAINT JOSEPHINE BAKHITA (1869–1947) Sister Bakhita is Sudan's first Catholic saint. Pope John Paul II canonized her (declared her a saint) in 2000. Bakhita was born in Darfur, and her birth name is unknown. Slave traders abducted her when she was nine and gave her the Arabic name Bakhita, meaning "lucky one." At fifteen she moved to Italy as the slave of an Italian trader. There she was baptized as Josephine, declared free, and became a nun. She spent her adult life teaching and caring for the poor.

OMAR HASSAN AL-BASHIR (b. 1944) Sudan's leader since 1989, al-Bashir was born in Shendi, south of Khartoum. His family were devout Muslims who lived along the Nile. He graduated from the Sudan Military College and served in the military, fighting against Israel and in southern Sudan. He became a general and associated with Hassan al-Turabi's National Islamic Front. Al-Bashir is a committed Islamist, believing that Sudanese politics and society should be guided by religion. A coup in 1989 brought him to power. In 2005 he signed a peace treaty to create a new government.

MANUTE BOL (b. 1962) Born in either Turalie or Gogrial, in southern Sudan, Bol is the son of a Dinka chief. Manute means "special blessing." He played basketball for Sudan's national team, then college basketball in the United States, where the National Basketball Association (NBA) recruited him to play. At 7 feet 7 inches tall (2.3 m), Bol is the tallest NBA player ever. He set a rookie record of 397 blocked shots during his first NBA season in 1985. In 1994 rheumatism forced him to retire. He gave most of his $3.5 million to the Sudanese People's Liberation Army.

JOHN GARANG (1945–2005) Garang, a Dinka, was born in the city of Bor in southern Sudan. He was described as charming, smart, and funny. He graduated with a degree in science from Grinnell College in Iowa in 1971, then returned to Sudan to join the southern rebels' cause. After the 1972 Machakos peace agreement, he became part of the Sudanese army. He returned to the United States and received a Ph.D. from Iowa State University in 1981. Two years later, he was back in Sudan when civil war broke out again. He left the army and became the leader of the SPLA. After the Comprehensive Peace Agreement between north and south, Garang became vice president in July 2005, but died in a helicopter crash three weeks later.

RAOUF MUSAD (b. 1937) Musad (also known as Moussad-Basta) was born in Port Sudan. He is an Arab playwright, journalist, and novelist. His parents were Egyptian Christians. This background is an important part of his struggle with identity and belonging, a theme in much of his writing. One of his many books is *Waiting for the Saviour: A Journey to the Holy Land*, published in 2000. In 2004 he started a small publishing company named Muhajiroun with other Arab writers living outside the Arab world. He lives in Amsterdam with his Dutch wife and their children.

MENDE NAZER (b. 1981) Nazer was born in the Nuba Mountains and grew up following traditional ways. When she was twelve, Arab raiders came to her village, killed most of the adults and stole many children, including Nazer. Slavers sold her to a wealthy Arab family in Khartoum. In 2000 the family sent her to serve as a household slave for an Arab Sudanese family in London. She escaped and told her story in the book *Slave: My True Story* (2003). She lives in London and speaks publicly about slavery in Sudan.

TAYEB SALIH (b. 1929) Born in northern Sudan, Salih attended school in Great Britain and has spent much of his life living abroad. He writes about political concerns such as colonization and the roles of women and men. Western and Arab literature, philosophy, and cultures mingle together in his works. He is best known for his novel *The Season of the Migration to the North*, published in 1967. Critics also consider him one of the best short-story authors writing in Arabic.

HASSAN AL-TURABI (b. 1932) Al-Turabi is the son of an Islamic judge and teacher. He became a leader of Islamist activists when he was a student at the University of Khartoum. He studied in London and Paris. By 1965 he was dean of the law school in Khartoum and formed what became the National Islamic Front. In Nimeiri's government, he was instrumental in the introduction of Sharia. Many considered him the main power behind President al-Bashir. However, the two struggled for control, and al-Bashir had al-Turabi arrested. In the summer of 2005, the government released al-Turabi as part of a general release of political prisoners.

Note: Little visited, Sudan is a destination for the adventurous. It has fascinating historical ruins and natural sights. Travelers report they are treated with great friendliness there. However, the U.S. Department of State warns against traveling to Sudan, and the government of Sudan has declared certain areas off limits to foreigners. See the State Department's website at http://travel.state.gov/travel/cis_pa_tw/tw/tw_934.html for updated travel warnings.

ANCIENT CUSH AND NUBIA The remains of Sudan's ancient Cushite cultures are north of Khartoum. The pyramids of the Royal Cemetery of Meroë are the most impressive of Sudan's archaeological sites. Nearby are several intact temples. Nubian archaeological sites farther north, around Dunquluh, include tomb wall paintings. The Lion Temple at Naqa has carvings of Apedemak, the lion god. Reaching these sites is an adventure in itself, as there is no public transportation. They are set among the scenic wonders of the Nile and the desert.

KASSALA Camel races on the plains west of Kassala draw large gatherings of nomads. You can buy Beja daggers or yards of bright material in Kassala's souks (markets). The granite Kassala hills form strange shapes, enticing hikers.

KHARTOUM The National Museum in Khartoum is the place to see treasures of Sudan's past, including temples rescued from the floodwaters of Lake Nasser. The large, silver-domed Mahdi's Tomb is a pilgrimage site worth seeing, though non-Muslims are not allowed inside. Boat trips up and down the Nile are a good way to see the modern city. The large and lively souk in Omdurman offers the sights, sounds, and smells of a traditional bazaar. On Fridays you can see Sufis dance and pray at sunset.

NUBA MOUNTAINS Green, rocky hills above the plains offer Sudan's most picturesque scenery and ideal hiking. The Nuba people are diverse and hospitable, but very poor. Visit in November when people hold autumn harvest festivals with feasting, wrestling, and dancing. Roads are minimal, and permits are required.

RED SEA COAST The clear, warm waters of the Red Sea offer some of the world's best deep-sea diving. Visitors can rent equipment in Port Sudan. Offshore coral reefs and their marine life are world-class. Divers can also visit ocean explorer Jacques Cousteau's *Conshelf II*, an abandoned experiment in underwater living.

Allah: Arabic for "God"

Arabic: the official language of Sudan. Classical Arabic is the language of the Quran.

bridewealth: a gift given by a groom to his future wife's family. Bridewealth is often cattle, but in modern times, it may be money or goods.

cataract: rapids, or a rocky stretch of river, difficult to navigate

desertification: the process of fertile land turning into desert, caused by a change of climate, a drought, or an overuse of dry lands

gross domestic product: the value of the goods and services produced by a country over a period of time, such as a year

Islam: a religion founded in the seventh century A.D. based on the teachings of the prophet Muhammad. There are two major Islamic sects, Shiite and Sunni. The holy book of Islam is the Quran.

Islamist: someone who wants Islam to be the basis for a country's entire society and the political state. Most Islamists work through peaceful means.

jallabiya: a long, loose robe worn by Arab men

Mahdi: in Islam an expected holy savior or liberator

mosque: an Islamic place of worship and prayer

Muslim: a follower of Islam

nomads: herders who move from place to place in search of pasture and water

oasis: a fertile place in the desert where underground water comes naturally to the surface

Quran: the holy book of Islam. The contents of the book were set forth by the prophet Muhammad starting in A.D. 610. Muslims believe that Allah revealed these messages to Muhammad through the angel Gabriel.

sanctions: trade restrictions that limit a country's imports and exports, imposed by one country to try to control or persuade another country

scarification: the practice of creating scar tattoos by making scratches or shallow cuts in the skin. These scar patterns are marks of identity and beauty.

Sharia: Islamic holy law

souk: Arabic for "marketplace," usually an open-air market

Sufi: follower of a mystical, spiritual branch of Islam. Sufis believe that individuals can have direct, personal knowledge of God.

Sunni: one of the two major Islamic sects, including about 90 percent of all Muslims. Sunnis follow Islamic leaders who are not chosen from Muhammad's direct relatives. Most Sudanese are Sunni.

Glossary

"Background Note: Sudan." *U.S. Department of State. Bureau of African Affairs.* **May 2005.**
http://www.state.gov/r/pa/ei/bgn/5424.htm (July 2005).
The site of the U.S. Department of State provides information about Sudan's people, government, economy, history, foreign relations, travel, and business.

BBC News (2005).
http://bbc.co.uk (August 10, 2005).
The online edition of the BBC (British Broadcasting Corporation) News is a good source for up-to-date coverage of Sudan.

Central Intelligence Agency (CIA). "Sudan." *The World Factbook.* **February 2005.**
http://www.cia.gov/cia/publications/factbook/geos/ly.html (March 20, 2005) .
The CIA's *World Factbook* provides maps, statistics, and basic information about Sudan's geography, people, government, economy, and more.

Clammer, Paul. *Sudan.* **Bucks, UK: Bradt Travel Guides, 2005.**
Clammer wrote this guide, one of the first modern travel guides to Sudan, after following the Nile through Sudan in 2002. He records the contrasts of the landscape, the variety of cultures, and the tradition of kindness to strangers that makes Sudan surprisingly hospitable for visitors.

"Documenting Atrocities in Sudan." *U.S. Department of State, Bureau of Public Affairs.* **September 2004.**
http://state.gov/g/drl/rls/36028.htm (May 4, 2005).
The survey data and final report of the Atrocities Documentation Team. The team conducted interviews in refugee camps in eastern Chad during the summer of 2004, interviewing 1,136 refugees who survived atrocities committed in the Darfur region.

The Economist. **2005.**
http://economist.com (May 2005).
This weekly British magazine, available online or in print editions, provides in-depth coverage of Sudan's economic and political news.

Knappert, Jan. *Kings, Gods and Spirits from African Mythology.* **New York: Peter Bedrick Books, 1986.**
Knappert is a leading expert on the languages and folklore of Africa. He retells different myths and legends from Africa, including Sudan, in this illustrated book. It is part of the World Mythology series.

Library of Congress, Federal Research Division. *Sudan: A Country Study.* **1991.**
http://countrystudies.us/Sudan/ (April 15, 2005).
This study presents the dominant social, political, economic, and military aspects of Sudanese society.

The Middle East and North Africa 2003. **London: Europa Publications Limited, 2002.**
The section on Sudan in this annual publication covers recent history, geography, culture, economy, politics, and government of the country. Statistics and sources are also included.

Selected Bibliography

Nazer, Mende, and Damien Lewis. *Slave: My True Story.* **New York: Public Affairs, 2003.**
With the help of a British journalist, Damien Lewis, Nazer wrote this book about her childhood with the Nuba and her life as a slave.

Parkinson, Tom. "Sudan." In David Else, et al., *Africa on a Shoestring.* **Footscray, Australia: Lonely Planet, 2004.**
Sudan is Africa's largest and least visited country. The chapter on Sudan in this African travel guidebook provides information on how to get to Sudan and what to see there. The author also provides some history and cultural background of the country.

Petterson, Donald. *Inside Sudan: Political Islam, Conflict, and Catastrophe.* **Boulder, CO: Westview Press, 1999.**
Petterson was the U.S. ambassador to Sudan from 1992 to 1995. This insightful book is about his experiences—both political and social—living in Khartoum and traveling to war-devastated southern Sudan.

Population Reference Bureau. **2004.**
http://www.prb.org (April 15, 2005).
The bureau offers current population figures, vital statistics, land area, and more. Special articles cover the environmental and health issues of Sudan.

Theroux, Paul. *Dark Star Safari: Overland from Cairo to Cape Town.* **Boston: Houghton Mifflin, 2003.**
On his journey overland from the north coast to the southern tip of Africa, Paul Theroux traveled through Sudan. A well-known travel writer, Theroux records his impressions of Khartoum, his trip into the desert to view pyramids half-buried in sand, and all sorts of men he meets.

Walgren, Judy. *The Lost Boys of Natinga: A School for Sudan's Young Refugees.* **Boston: Houghton Mifflin, 1998.**
Walgren, an American photojournalist, traveled to the Natinga refugee camp for children in southern Sudan. With photos and interviews, she documents the children's hardships and struggles for education.

Waller, John H. *Gordon of Khartoum: The Saga of a Victorian Hero.* **New York: Macmillan, 1988.**
A sympathetic biography of the nineteenth-century British military and diplomatic figure, General Charles Gordon, who, the author says, some see as a hero and some as a lunatic. Gordon's career—and his life—ended in Khartoum, where the Mahdi's forces trapped him. A British expedition arrived too late to save Gordon, who was killed when Khartoum fell on January 26, 1885.

Aboulela, Leila. *The Translator*. Edinburgh, UK: Polygon, 2001.
Contrasting the landscapes and culture of Sudan and Scotland, this novel is about Sammar, a young Sudanese widow who works in a university in Scotland. As she recovers from the grief of her husband's death, she finds her friendship with an older professor turning to love. But their cultural differences are huge, and Sammar does not want to lose her traditions.

Ali, Idris. *Dongola: A Novel of Nubia*. Translated by Peter Theroux. Fayetteville: University of Arkansas Press, 1999.
Idris Ali is a well-known Sudanese author. This novel about Dongola (also spelled Dunqulah), an ancient Nubian capital along the Nile, is one of relatively few Sudanese books to be translated into English. The author tells a story of divided cultures, lost lands, impossible dreams, and abandoned loves.

Bok, Francis. *Escape from Slavery: The True Story of My Ten Years in Slavery—and My Journey to Freedom in America*. New York: St. Martin's Press, 2003.
In this modern slave narrative, Francis Bok, a Christian Dinka, relates how Arab raiders abducted him, when he was seven years old. Sold into slavery, he lived with the goats and cattle he tended. His owner told him, "You are an animal." Bok ran away to Khartoum when he was seventeen. Eventually reaching the United States as a refugee, he works to end slavery around the world. In this book, Bok also writes about the Dinka culture and the history of Sudan.

Deng, Benson, Alephonsion Deng, and Benjamin Ajak. *They Poured Fire on Us from the Sky*. New York: Public Affairs, 2005.
This is a collection of essays by the Deng brothers and their cousin Benjamin. The three were under seven years old when their Dinka villages were attacked during the civil war. In 2001 they came to the United States and began to write. Refugee life, they recall, was "like being devoured by wild animals."

Diagram Group. *Peoples of North Africa*. New York: Facts on File, 1997.
This book is part of the Peoples of Africa series. It presents the different cultures and traditions of the major ethnic groups of North Africa, including the Arabs, Dinka, and Nuba people of Sudan. Drawings, charts, and maps highlight the text.

Levy, Patricia. *Sudan*. New York: Marshall Cavendish, 1997.
Part of the Cultures of the World series, this book covers geography, history, economy, lifestyle, and more about Sudan. It is well illustrated with photos and maps.

***Lost Boys of Sudan*. Directed by Mylan, Megan, and Jon Shenk. New Group Video, 2004. DVD or VHS.**
Lost Boys of Sudan—first shown on the PBS series *P.O.V.* in 2003—is a documentary film about two Dinka boys orphaned by civil war in Sudan, who walked to refugee camps in Kenya. Their journey continued in 2001, when they were resettled in Houston, Texas. The film focuses on their efforts—sometimes funny, sometimes sad—to establish lives and gain education to help their friends and home country.

Lugira, Aloysius M. *African Religion*. New York: Facts on File, 1999.
This book for young adults looks at the main elements of African religions. It

explains that the central points of African religion are a belief in a supreme being, the existence of the spirit world, and that all things in the universe and the human community are interconnected, part of a whole.

Mason, A. E. W. *The Four Feathers.* **New York: Simon & Schuster, 2002.**
This classic adventure tale set in Sudan was first published in Great Britain in 1902. The hero, British officer Harry Feversham, resigns from the army in 1882. At the same time, his regiment is sent to war in Sudan. Receiving white feathers—symbols of cowardice—Harry goes undercover to Sudan to prove his bravery. The tale has been translated to film, most recently in 2002.

Riefenstahl, Leni. *The Last of the Nuba.* **New York: St. Martin's Press, 1973.**
This book of photography records the traditional ways of some of the one hundred different ethnic groups who live in the Nuba Mountains. Body art and wrestling are featured, as are everyday life.

Salih, Tayeb. *The Season of the Migration to the North.* **Oxford, UK: Heinemann, 1969.**
Tayeb Salih is one of the Arab world's most important writers. This book, his most famous novel, is a tale of life along the Nile in northern Sudan.

"Sudan." *University of Pennsylvania, African Studies Center.*
http://www.sas.upenn.edu/African_Studies/Country_Specific/Sudan.html
The African Studies Center at the University of Pennsylvania offers many links to find information about Sudan, concerning everything from comic books to human rights abuses.

"Sudan Information Gateway." *United Nations System in Sudan.*
http://www.unsudanig.org/
This site offers access to information about the United Nations in Sudan. The UN operates throughout Sudan, to identify and focus upon priority areas for humanitarian, recovery, and developmental interventions.

Sudan Net.
http://sudan.net
This site offers general information concerning Sudan and links to the latest news from the country.

vgsbooks.com
http://www.vgsbooks.com
Visit vgsbooks.com, the home page of the Visual Geography Series®, which is updated regularly. You can get linked to all sorts of useful online information, including geographical, historical, demographic, cultural, and economic websites. The vgsbooks.com site is a great resource for late-breaking news and statistics.

Zwier, Lawrence J. *Sudan: North against South.* **Minneapolis: Lerner Publications Company, 1999.**
Part of the World in Conflict series, this book uncovers what was behind the fighting between government troops and southern rebel groups. Zwier also discusses the main players and the attempts to achieve peace. The book is well-illustrated with historical drawings, photos, and maps. The ample and clear information provides a good background for understanding Sudan.

Captions for photos appearing on cover and chapter openers:

Cover: Pyramids from the ancient Cushitic civilization are found in northern Sudan.

pp. 4–5 A woman gathers firewood in a grassy field in eastern Sudan.

pp. 8–9 The White Nile provides water for irrigation near the city of Kusti.

pp. 20–21 The largest site of Cush civilization burial pyramids lies north of Khartoum, along the Nile River in ancient Meroë.

pp. 36–37 A Sudanese family stands outside their home in eastern Sudan.

pp. 46–47 Muslims from the north of Sudan pray together.

pp. 58–59 Sugarcane is an important crop of Sudan. This sugar estate is comprised of fields and a factory for processing sugar.

Photo Acknowledgments
The images in this book are used with the permission of: © Helene Rogers/Art Directors, pp. 4–5, 8–9, 10, 36–37, 38–39, 58–59; © XNR Productions, pp. 6, 11; © Jeremy Hartley/Panos Pictures, p. 13; © Silvio Fiore/SuperStock, p. 15; © ZSSD/SuperStock, p. 17; © Anthony Ham/Lonely Planet Images, p. 18; © Jonathan Blair/CORBIS, pp. 20–21; © Mary Evans Pictures Library, p. 25; © Bettmann/CORBIS, p. 28; U.S. Agency for International Development, pp. 31, 32–33; © Reuters/CORBIS, p. 32; © Thomas Mukoya/Reuters/CORBIS, p. 35; © Liba Taylor/CORBIS, p. 38; © John Robinson/MCC/Global Aware, p. 40; © Time Life Pictures/Getty Images, p. 41; Kay Chernush/Agency for International Development, pp. 42, 60; © Hartmut Schwarzbach/Peter Arnold, Inc., p. 43; © Sven Torfinn/Panos Pictures, pp. 46–47; Erich Lessing/Art Resource, NY, p. 50; © Getty Images, p. 51; © Caroline Penn/Panos Pictures, p. 52; © Penny Tweedie/CORBIS, p. 53; © Wendy Stone/CORBIS, p. 55; © David Clegg/Art Directors, p. 61; Agency for International Development, p. 63; Audrius Tomonis–www.banknotes.com, p. 68.

Front cover: © Michael S. Yamashita/CORBIS. Back cover: NASA.